RELEASE THE BUTTERFLY

A Manifesto for Change in the Studio

Robert Murray Diefendorf

Butterfly Press
Princeton, New Jersey

Release the Butterfly

Published by Butterfly Press
150 John Street
Princeton, New Jersey 08542
www.releasethebutterfly.com

Editorial: Steve Carlson, Maria Penelope Mannas Diefendorf
Printing: Transcontinental Printing—Book Group
Typography: Robert Goodman, Silvercat™, San Diego, California
Cover Design, Illustration, Logo: Samantha Wall

First Printing

Publisher's Cataloging-in-Publication
(provided by Stan Szalewicz)

Diefendorf, Robert Murray.
Release the butterfly : a manifesto for change in the
studio / Robert Murray Diefendorf. — 1st ed.
p. cm.
Includes glossary.
LCCN: 2003091285
ISBN: 0-9729887-0-X

I. Piano—Instruction and study. I. Title.

MT 220.D54 2003 786.2'193 21

Printed on acid-free paper in Canada

To Penni, my wife
My love my life
Whose tireless efforts, spacious soul
and unique insights
Made this book possible.

CONTENTS

Acknowledgements

To my parents for teaching me how to live and believe.

To my family, old and new, for their love.

To Ena Bronstein Barton and Scott Hoerl for their faith.

To Carl C. Atteniese, Jr. and Corinne Glassman for being there.

To Christine Casati for her spirit.

To Sonia Mehta for her insight.

To the readers and professionals who contributed to and helped me write this book, especially Adelaide McKelway and Ilene Dube.

To my students, with whom this book begins and ends.

FOREWORD

Just when I was flailing about with desperate cries of "where have all the great teachers gone?" (higher education can do that to you), just as the bombs over a multitude of human spaces are beginning to drop and multiply, you send me this (which I have printed out and bound for myself), that gets me back to the papers I need to write, the book that's burning inside me- and the absolute certainty I have now that I will learn music!

Your book spoke very deeply to me. I study pedagogy, I love to teach, teaching is where I live and breathe. I feel very privileged that you sent this my way. Your book is like a window into your soul, it is nakedly honest, an achingly human account (with ordinary need and extraordinary struggle) of the creation of knowledge that starts from gifts that we own and ultimately depends on the connections we make with each other and with those gifts.

I would recommend this book to anyone, in fact, embarking on a process of study, student and teacher, because it is a metaphor for all sustained learning which then becomes a connection to self and lived lives. There is much here I wish my teachers had known, much I see as my own capacity as student, and more that I can give as a teacher.

Unlike most books that deal with "feeling success" or "how-to," your book demonstrates deep spirituality transcending the barriers so often placed between theory and practice. I was ready to say, at some point, I am not a student of music, this will depart from my experience essentially; but no, essentially, it stayed with me and I know I will pick it up again, many times.

It is very seldom that one comes across a book on pedagogy or method that does not slide into abstractions and pompousness, and that's why this book is like a gift that resonates with that core human condition, which the book does not allow one to forget. In fact, this is a book I would ask students of literature, sociology and education to read at the outset of their studies. Not least at all, to teachers too; this book is a pathway into the soul (whatever the state of that soul) towards that deep, sometimes submerged place of complex meaning in each individual self. And you do this with such uncluttered, simple prose that is fluid to read.

This book can be read in bits or at a stretch (I have done both). In bits (or at stages), it assumes an immediacy and potency that is useful as well as delightful. At a stretch, it is like a journey into a way of knowing-

and this happens because you have the great felicity of picking up thoughts and ideas that follow from the previous sections.

I must tell you that I now have privileged knowledge of the most magical kind that *Release the Butterfly* has given me. I feel privileged in fact to know you (so you can imagine how I feel about asking to comment!). I feel the deep embrace of music, loss and struggle, passion and of course joy. All education is waiting for a book like this. I know a multitude that I would ask to read this book. It reminds me in part, of *Zen and the Art of Motorcycle Maintenance*, in part of *An Equal Music*, in part of *Hamlet's Dresser*, all different books, all events in themselves.

But even if I had read none of these, your book would reach my core — and stay with me, as it has. There are others in education circles who write on pedagogy, like bell hooks of the minority experience in schools, and so on. For me, music pedagogy becomes the process that could inform all of these fields because they sometimes leave out: beauty, joy and spirituality.

It's a work of great love, Bob. My very deepest thanks for the privilege of reading it.

Godspeed,
Sonia Mehta, PhD.,
Studies in Global Education,
from letter to author

How to Use This Book

❧ Goal

This book is about positive change in learning. It is as full of fresh perspectives and new ideas in piano pedagogy as I could muster.

While I don't claim to always be right, I hope everything sparks a thought, discussion or argument!

❧ Why Butterfly?

I have used the butterfly's stages of change, from eggs on a leaf, to caterpillar, to shedding skins, to cocoon, to flight, as a model for growth. A butterfly makes a dramatic and extreme transformation, starting as a slow-moving caterpillar and ending up a symbol of beauty and freedom.

❧ Glossary for Transformation

Words used throughout book that deal with change.

❧ List of Professionals

Quick reference of professionals, both in and out of the music field, consulted for the book.

❧ Index, Bibliography

And other features related to book can be found at releasethebutterfly.com. Please submit your ideas related to any of the topics in question. Instructions for submission are at website.

INTRODUCTION

The life cycle of the butterfly is arguably one of the most bizarre and impressive examples of nature at work on the planet — one could be forgiven for believing that caterpillars and butterflies were entirely separate species.

～ The Amazing Lifecycle of a Butterfly
http://www.butterflies.org.uk/
lbh_home/cycle/lifecycl.htm

Dramatic change, as in the life of the butterfly, has been a trademark of my musical life, pedagogical life, and life in general. As in the quote above, I hope I am forgiven for thinking at times that the crawling caterpillar that I am in many departments may someday fly. I would hate to think that I am defined by weaknesses. Rather, I like the idea that weaknesses can be overcome, gracefully, with purple and gold wings.

This book is less a guide to teaching piano than it is a love-letter to our students' musical souls, an invitation to come out, play, sing and dance. It asks the questions: How did we get there, both in our lives and in musical study, and how can we pass it on? And it is a portrait of teachers as guides, shamans, artists and observers of humanity, nature and the divine.

Sometimes I like to stop a lesson briefly and point to the dappled sunlight splashed across the wall, golden and waning. Or in the evening, the way the branches make creepy, over-sized silhouettes on the blinds. These are reminders to students and myself to be present, to notice the simple and beautiful details of our environment, and then bring the same immediacy and beauty to our music.

In the same way, with this book, I would like to stop and point to some ideas related to change in our studios.

The idea that we can perceive all students as fine musicians. The idea that state of mind directly impacts our studio. The idea that students have physical and spiritual "habits" that can be transformed into more positive ones. The idea that the word "talent" is limiting and that all students are blessed with many varied talents. The idea that artistry is available to all students who want it, and who are willing to look at the creepy shadows and try to recreate them.

If through this short book I can provide my gentle readers with some new perspectives and ideas, I will be honored.

Thank you for your precious time.

NOTES ON POLITICALLY CORRECT GRAMMAR

I use the pronoun "I" instead of "you" or "we" as much as possible, because I like to speak only for myself. I alternate my use of "he" with "she," sometimes even on the same page. I know many "old-schoolers" object to this and prefer the grammatically correct "he" throughout, but I am bending towards politically correct times. As a teacher, I believe in the power of words and the example I show through my choices. In case you haven't noticed, I often use contractions, when it's more natural to do so. I have read the classics and hold Strunk and White's *The Elements of Style* in high regard, but since this book is more meditational than scholarly, it would seem a bit forced to spell out all words. Finally, I often use the phrase "the student must" or "the student should" or "I, as the teacher, must..." Please understand that I never pretend to know what must happen in any learning situation. I only offer what I believe should happen if the student and teacher desire musical, philosophical and spiritual growth.

EGG STAGE:
WHY, WHO AND HOW?

The mother butterfly "tastes" plants for suitability, using her legs. The plant must be chemically compatible with her species so the young larvae can feed on it. After laying the eggs, the mother leaves, never to see her young.

The mother butterfly must seek a plant with the right shape, color and biochemical make-up. She must find the right one so that when the egg hatches and the larva emerges, it may feed on that plant. Finding the right match for a plant is therefore the first step in becoming a butterfly.

~ Unknown Web Site

My transformation as a piano student, pianist or teacher must begin with a basic understanding of why I play the piano, where I am, acceptance, and willingness to change.

LIKE A DREAM, IT FOLLOWS ME

When I first lived in New York City, I worked at a restaurant near Central Park. Walking from the subway, I
used to pass a man who played an old upright piano on
the sidewalk near the noisy, frenetic entrance to Central
Park. I learned from a friend that he lived on the street.

For a year or so he disappeared. When he returned,
he had a grand piano. This served as shelter when he
slept. In rain or snow he covered it with plastic. He
would play touchingly mad strains of music that
floated up between the buildings like lost balloons,
echoing after me like a reminder of what I had left behind. I had just graduated from music school, and was
trying with all my might to give up music.

One night my co-worker friend and I sat at an outdoor café on Broadway, across from Lincoln Center
and the Metropolitan Opera. It was a gentle summer
evening. The fountain gushed opulently, and con-
cert-goers swanned across the plaza. Our "outdoor pianist" had moved closer to the action and was playing
and nodding at people walking by.

"Is he really good, Bob?" my friend asked me. I was slightly shocked and embarrassed. I'd been trying to maintain a disguise as a bartender and leave behind my own young and wrinkled past in classical music. "I mean, you really know about this. Is he just crazy?"

Across the street, the lights burned in the lobby of Avery Fisher Hall. I pictured the Philharmonic members gathered backstage, thought about the hours and years each of them had spent in basement practice rooms all over the world. With my eyes I lazily followed Juilliard students, walking to their rooms at the seedy Westside YMCA. They were red in the face, exhausted, carrying violins and backpacks, looking slightly ticked off.

I thought of Schumann in the asylum, Chopin at Majorca, Scriabin's unearthly melodies, Horowitz playing octave scales over and over in the middle of the day in his beach house with the shades down, and my own life.

"No," I said after a pause.

We continued eating, and moved onto other topics.

THIS PLANT WAS CHOSEN.
WHY PIANO?

Morning; I look at the piano. What a strange object. A big box, a bench in front, a row of buttons. Inside, levers and joints, strings. How did we choose it as a place to spend so much of our time?

I sit at the piano. The bench is hard, wooden, the keys cool, smooth. I press one down; it makes a sound, an isolated pitch arcing out into the room. How did Beethoven's opus 109 come out of this? How did Horowitz make all those roaring, singing sounds? How did my student, only last night, play Nancy Faber's *Nocturne* with such passion and unique style?

I tell my students, we are part of this machine. It does not exist as an instrument without us. It is like a singer's vocal cords — waiting for the blast of air from the diaphragm. We are an important half of this total instrument. Perhaps it is helpful to rename it. The original name of this instrument was *pianoforte-* an Italian compound word meaning *soft-loud*, shortened by most people to *piano*. Maybe we should call it *pianohumano*. *Piano Human*.

So, by adjusting the humano part of the pianohumano, by wriggling around, rotating and twisting the arms and wrists, and moving the hands in relation to the keys, I can make infinite spatial relationships with the piano part of the pianohumano. Thus, its construction changes every day, every second. The humano part is composed mostly of water, so it changes with the weather, with my mood, with my age.

Then remember how many humanos there are— everyone, from eighteen months old to one hundred and forty-five years young will have a different sound. They will create, with their touch, a different total instrument.

So maybe this box, these cool, yellowing ivories are not so strange or inhospitable. Maybe the sound is very natural.

I warm-up with a slow, one-octave scale, c-sharp minor. Somehow the keys feel so natural against me, against the sound. I push in the way only I can do. It pushes back, recognizing me. This piano, invented only three hundred years ago, seems as part of me as my bones. Part of my DNA evolution. I am grateful for this invention.

I play Bach's Prelude to his a minor English Suite. The music is noble, knowing, and majestic. At times, it is questioning, and then it evades the question and weaves itself into more questions, somehow also answers. The counterpoint and imitation create what seems to be a living organism, full of doubts, worries, sudden strengths, triumphs, and more questions.

As the piece progresses, the word pianohumano becomes even more apt. The piano and music create moments that more than mirror the human condition, they seem to create human moments unto themselves. And through Bach's exquisite pianism, the hands feel so right. The combination of feel and sound and music make sense in a way that does more than address or reflect something I already know in my life. It states a new context, a new universe, and then answers it. I am in awe. Again, I am thankful.

The piece is over. I sit, thinking and feeling: "Yes." As an artist, and a human, I wonder if anyone heard it and went to the same places with me, understood my voyage, was awed by what Bach just did, not three hundred years ago, but just now, in my studio. I listen. Nobody's around. But I heard, and still can't believe my ears.

I start the piece again. When I am done, I am no closer to the mystery of what Bach did with the keyboard than before. But I am exhilarated. I was the humano part of the pianohumano, the performer of the old masterpiece.

I didn't write the piece, I didn't even play it perfectly, but it just stood up on the page and jumped off and told us of its tragedies and triumphs, thanks to my hands. And it really was a live spark, a burning ember that Bach wrapped in a blanket so long ago, in a way that he knew would never die. As long as there are pianofortes to sit in front of in the cold morning and humanos to unwrap the ember.

THE EGG STAGE

✿ Past Becomes Present...

Each of us is a collection of experiences, thoughts, emotions and habits. Everything that has happened to us helps to shape us and leaves a scar or a chip. Or sometimes knocks an entire stone out of our foundation. Or, to see things positively, adds a colorful marking of some kind. As pianists and teachers, our musical past also leaves its mark, at times subtly, other times in more painfully obvious ways.

✿ The Egg Stage

It is important to realize that the "missing stones" in my foundation, either as a person or as an artist, can often be replaced. And it can be exciting, as well as exhausting.

The moment I decide to assess where I am with a view to change, I am at the egg stage of my transformation. It will hatch, grow and fly, but this first requires attention.

14

✌ Where Are My Egg Stages?

At times I feel frustrated in my teaching and playing. In the past I have had these complaints, and more:

- Learning new repertoire has taken too long.
- My tone was flat and wooden.
- At times I have not been able to get my students to practice.
- I have had trouble making a piece "sing."

I have also dealt with personal "gaps":

- I have been afraid of dealing with people (causing stagnation in jobs and sometimes social isolation).
- I have tended to leave projects and jobs when they become too difficult or intimidating, or they threaten to show my weaknesses.

I have struggled with these, and many other "egg stages." Some times it was necessary to find out why they had never hatched. Other times it was a matter of finding the right person to help me nurture them. Always it led back to the same idea: that I need to take responsibility for making them grow. Some have grown into healthy young larvae and have flown away. Others are still crawling. Either way, the process was always exciting and empowering.

❧ Acknowledgement and Acceptance

The first step in progress is always acceptance. One of the biggest obstacles to "fixing" what is wrong or even identifying it in the first place is the fear of exposure, that I will be "found out."

But the more experience I gain, the more I realize that professionals are constantly sharing their weaknesses and flaws. Piano teachers I admire greatly and who have substantial reputations admit a variety of these weaknesses, from not being able to play this piece, to almost being burned out, to not understanding a certain level of theory. And it's fine. They are still great teachers and musicians.

If I admit that I need to change, it means I want to change, and that can only be good — not scary or embarrassing.

So, I accept where I am as a teacher and musician, and who I am as a person. I forget about where I should be. Instead, I focus on where I'm going.

❧ Some Questions

How do I find out where I am as a teacher, musician, and human? The first step in progress is always asking questions and confronting issues.

Some questions, like fear of driving, can be discussed and dismissed over coffee with a friend.

Others, like financial management and work ethic, require concentrated effort and discipline. For some questions, professional help was required, either through continued piano study or personal and professional counseling. But they all required that I first want to improve and that I take responsibility for what's lacking.

Of course I didn't ask or answer these all at once. Certain events had to happen and certain realizations take place before I even asked some of these questions. But when I did, more questions would come and with them, more answers and more directions to go for help.

❧ Start with Foundation of Faith

Although the questions sometimes have no immediate answers and can be contradictory, I start from the assumption that I am acting out of love and a desire to change. I act from a position of faith that my goal or mission is good and correct. Thus, the mission itself does not get questioned, only how to carry it out.

Lewis Mehl-Madrona, M.D., author of *Coyote Medicine*, western doctor and shaman, says that a healer needs to create an image of wellness. He needs to believe in this image and make the patient believe in it.

I believe a teacher has the same obligation to a student. I never allow a student to accept an image of himself that reflects less than his potential. I always show him what beautiful music is possible, and promise him that if he is willing, I can help him make those sounds himself.

So, accept where you are, where your own particular egg stage is. Then, like the mother butterfly who knows intuitively where to lay her eggs, have faith that they will find nourishment from the plant you have chosen, then grow, hatch, and eventually fly.

WHO DO I WANT TO BE?

The larval stage of a butterfly's life, commonly known as the caterpillar, reaches a point where he must shed his exoskeleton. He usually does this four times before spinning the cocoon, where he will transform into a butterfly.

Later, when the butterfly emerges from the cocoon, his wings are still wet from metamorphosing. He pumps a special red liquid into the veins in his wings, again, literally pushing his body to become the right size and shape. Then he dries the wings in the sun and flies away. The whole process, from caterpillar to flight, happens without any parental supervision.

I like to believe that I too can "shed skins," blow my persona to fit into the biggest skin I can imagine, then finally pump blood into my wings and fly. This example in nature is especially poignant because the caterpillar achieves change by *force of personal will*, with instinct playing a role, of course.

❧ Who Do I Want To Be?

Once I have realized "where my eggs have been laid" (in music, on the piano!) and then assessed where I am, the question becomes who do I want to be? What experiences and habits do I want to keep? What habits do I encourage my students to keep or lose?

Often we apply labels to ourselves and others, naming ourselves after past events in our lives or our patterns. We say that the student is *unmusical*, but has he ever been taught proper phrasing? We say the teacher is *disorganized*, but has he ever been taught to budget his time?

We are limited only by the false notion that we cannot change. Instead of accepting limits, I seek answers to the beautiful question: *How can I become who I want to be?*

THE CATERPILLAR'S FIRST SKIN:
REMOVE PRECONCEPTIONS

As caterpillars grow, their exoskeleton becomes tight on them, so they molt (lose their old exoskeleton). After the molt, while the new skin is still soft, they swallow a lot of air, which expands their body. Then, when the cuticle hardens, they let the air out and have room for growth.

> ➤ Enchantedlearning.com
> http://www.enchantedlearning.com/subjects/butterfly/

The caterpillar will shed its skin, or molt, as it grows, to accommodate the larger size.

> ➤ Life Cycle of a Butterfly, Bellevue State Park Website
> http://www.state.ia.us/parks/lifecycl.htm

Often stagnation comes when I hold onto negative beliefs. When my mind is open to new beliefs, I can begin to grow.

BEGINNER MIND

I think of "beginner's mind" as the mind that faces life like a small child, full of curiosity and wonder and amazement. "I wonder what this is? I wonder what that is? I wonder what this means?" Without approaching things with a fixed point of view or a prior judgement, just asking, "what is it?"

~ Abbess Zenkei Blanche Hartman, on the phrase "beginner's mind," first used by Shunryu Suzuki
From *Chapel Hill Zen Center* website
http://www.intrex.net/chzg/ hartman4.htm

I adopted the philosophy *beginner mind* very early in my teaching, before I had really heard it as a Zen phrase. I simply decided that anyone could teach me something:

- ⚹ the youngest student
- ⚹ his three-year-old brother
- ⚹ his grandmother
- ⚹ my director
- ⚹ a seasoned pedagogue
- ⚹ or even a neophyte teacher, like myself at the time.

I decided to put aside my ego and pride and just be open. My first few weeks in a classroom were an education in being humble. I taught music history in a gifted program and many of the students were prima donas. They made it very clear that my class was an unwanted requirement. Much of my time was spent getting their attention, stopping them from drawing, talking, or trying to play their instruments.

Many different people helped me gain mastery over the subtleties of classroom teaching. One was Heather, a precocious twelve-year-old in the class, who would shout out pedagogical advice in the heat of battle. The class would be spinning out of control and she would say loudly above the din: "Just start and they'll shut up!" And other equally blunt but enlightening suggestions that worked. Or I would call up the director, Scott Hoerl, and ask how to deal with a certain parent or situation. He would sit me down and spell out exactly how to proceed.

As a young person, being open to suggestions from all quarters had been difficult for me. Taking criticism was something I was not good at, and I interpreted almost any suggestion as criticism. Thus, I did not allow myself to be open to new ideas and information, or other people's experience. I limited my own progress, and I had a rough time pursuing goals. Either I fumbled along by myself, or when I did accept advice or tutelage, I frequently became depressed or stopped the activity, afraid.

By opening myself to any source, I can grow exponentially. I am blessed to work alongside very accomplished pedagogues. Of course their ideas are invaluable. But even a child can give me useful information, if her particular experience has given her a perspective I could never have.

It's important to develop one's own ideas and become discriminating. But I still hold this to be true: treat every day as though it were my first day teaching, and treat everybody like world famous experts on teaching, music or life, who might tell me something I need. Because they are and they can.

Students as the Expression of My Soul

❦ I Am My Students

I never want to have only just one type of student in the studio, or even one level or motivation level.

My students' challenges represent to me my relationship with my own musical intellect. The solutions we've found together show the ways in which I have grown as a teacher: my insight, analytical ability, listening.

Their personalities and spirit represent my relationship with my own soul and with the world. I leave the studio each year a new and improved human.

❦ Each Student as a New Universe

One of the most intriguing moments for me in a student's career is when I first see him sit at the piano. This is my first glimpse into his musical universe. He immediately has his own sound, style and body language. At that first moment, we see what we are all blessed with. And it's not just in the hands — it's in the eyes, the glow in the face, and how he reacts to the creation of sound.

Even at that first moment, he is already a unique musical individual, with an infinite potential for developing his own tastes, sensibilities, unique palate of sonorities, and personal interpretation. For the teacher, this is a world of listening, and finding new ways to convey ideas. For the students, it is a world they can build and furnish for themselves over a lifetime.

My studio has been a melting pot of the most delicious order. It has included:

- those who needed free lessons
- those whose houses resembled a public library
- students who hated piano and me
- those who loved me but hated piano
- those who loved piano and hated me
- students from Guatemala, Mexico, mainland China, Hong Kong, Korea, France, and other nations
- many races and religions
- the affluent city, the inner city
- the affluent and middle-American suburbs
- students from three years old to eighty-three
- students with great musical talent
- those with learning challenges

⤳ and some with behavioral challenges.

And every single one has made me a better teacher, by offering something different that relates to the whole.

♭ Unconventional Talents

Not every student has been "talented on paper." But they have all had their own unique talents that I believe will someday translate into profound and beautiful music-making.

For example, there's Milton, a fifth-grade boy who is precociously verbal and shares his day with me at lessons, bubbling over with joy and excitement. When he conquers his rhythm and technique, and masters a Liszt *Hungarian Rhapsody,* it will be all fire!

Then there's Julia, a nine-year-old girl who has plenty of work to do on "jellyfish fingers." Her gifts are bravery and toughness. If she sticks with it and gets the hands and sound more uniform, she could play a Romantic concerto or Chopin etudes, or some piece designed for warriors only.

Susan, a high school student, sees connections between spirituality, science and music, and loves to practice only a few pieces, but in depth. She has intellectual and musical curiosity to a high degree and we can really go into the psychological, cultural and harmonic aspects of a piece. When she starts playing late Beethoven sonatas, they will be like fine wine.

And so forth.

Students' Weaknesses that Hone our Teaching Craft

More important than the students' strengths are their weaknesses and faults.

If a student were a perfect model of learning, receptive and willing, hardworking and musically gifted, and with perfect character and upright spirit, I would only use some of my teaching powers. For example, sharing ideas and demonstrating love for piano.

But I would never have the occasion to do a thousand things that make teaching an exhilarating and creative experience. I wouldn't have to confront a student on her work ethic, I wouldn't have to find ways to motivate her, inspire her to change this or that, find ways to convince her of this new technique. I would never have to phrase a suggestion in a different way. I would never have to consider the student's character and spiritual way of being, because those personal attributes would be perfect.

Students as Soul

My students inform the parameters of my teaching and human soul. They chip it, crack it, cry into it, embrace it, push it away, live in it, love and also leave it. I am a more complete person because of them.

Inviting a universe of unique students into my studio exercises two of my most important skills as a teacher: acceptance and compassion.

We need the prodigies, the competition winners, and the future concert pianists. We need these extraordinary players to bring us exquisite renditions of Mozart.

But we also need students who struggle, who have obstacles, and who want to discover the beauty they hold within.

TURNAROUND

❧ The Sins of Labeling

Often students are seen as certain types of learners. If you are faint of heart and very nurturing, better to skip this next paragraph. I include it only as examples of what some teachers, parents and students themselves use to describe piano students. My point is to eliminate these words from the discussion, but I would like to put them out there first, like dusty stained old items that you dredge up from the basement and line up in the yard before hosing them down or hauling them to the dump.

- Teachers talk about the *star*, the one who plays at the end of recitals, enters competitions, and for whom audiences always clap, gasp, and look at each other in amazement.
- They also talk about *hacks, duds, dogs,* and more.
- They talk about the talented, the untalented, the average student, the lazy student, the unmusical student, the *talker*, and the *banger*.

I know, those are insensitive and even cruel words. But I often hear piano teachers use these words and others to describe the students who often can't remember where middle *C* is after three years of lessons, never learn to put hands together, or, if they do progress at all, do so with the utmost patience we can muster.

But using labels, even in our own minds, can damage them as pianists and students and limit us as teachers.

And the worst sin of all is acting on the labels we give to students, even if unspoken.

❧ "No Dogs..."

A few years ago a colleague of mine was praising a third teacher. This third teacher was a type herself, whom I call a *bigwig*. She had had a concert career in Europe, had trained at the best conservatories there, spoke with a foreign accent, and, in short, intimidated the varnish off my piano. My friend made the comment that the bigwig "didn't have any dogs," meaning all her students were at least competent. She went on to say that the bigwig treated all students like they could achieve some success, and, as a result, they did.

That stuck with me. What if I could have that attitude?

❧ Disclaimer

Obviously there are always students who defy the curve and simply want to do X when everything in your being wants them to do Z. I once had a mother who said, "Piano for my children is just below sorting socks on their priority list." This is difficult to confront.

But in general, if you interview students and parents carefully, you will have students and parents who agree with your philosophy.

❧ Turnaround

I do have one term that I use, if only because it is really not a type as much as a philosophy. The word is *turnaround*, which applies to students who enter with one preconceived notion about themselves and, after a few months, gain another, more positive one.

A favorite turnaround story of mine was a girl called Beena. My school, where I teach once a week, assigned her to me. She was a classic example of the callous label: *retread*. These students go through several teachers, never practicing or trying in the lessons, just marking time until the latest teacher "cries uncle" and passes them along. Then they go to a new teacher and repeat the process. I was next on the list, I guess. But I surprised her, I think.

On my first lesson I asked who her last teacher was and recognized the name as someone who has little patience for this kind of student. I leafed through her assignment notebook and — yep! — as if on cue, there were the classic signs of a teacher giving up on a student, perfunctory notes with little or no commentary. I asked her to play for me, and the classic answers came. I haven't really played over the summer, the teacher never put me in a recital, I didn't like my piece, on and on. Finger pointing and excuses.

I assessed what her weaknesses were and "prescribed" the right "medicine:" some Hanon here, some scales there, a Baroque piece, and she picked out a pop song she liked. Every week she would practice only the piece she liked and ignore the rest. Confronting her negligence, I asked her if she wanted to play the piano. She said yes. To be sure, she liked her pop piece a lot and I could sense she wanted to play well, but wanted nothing to do with the process it took to get there. *Treating her as if she were any good student* was proving to be difficult, but I was determined to do that.

After a month or so of getting nowhere, I asked her if she believed the instructions I put in the notebook would actually help her. Rather apathetically, shrugging her shoulders, she said, "Not really. I don't know." Swift came my reply: "Well, I can't teach any other way." I followed it up with one of those steely glances you don't like to pull out of the bag too often. Immediately the apathy drained from her eyes, replaced by vague concern and a look of possible conciliation.

The next few weeks she tried more and more. Slowly but surely her sense of detailed study was improving. With technical work, her hand position and strength were improving. I could see in her face something missing in the first lessons- a sense of pride. She was actually getting better. One lesson near the end of the fall term was the turning point, I think.

We were polishing a piece that was to be played that weekend in our winter recital (her first ever, she insisted!). She still had problem spots that she just hadn't fixed. We took the entire lesson and worked in minute detail on each small section, mastering one measure, then the next, then two in a row, and so on. Finally, she played it through, without a stop. Wide-eyed, she said breathlessly, "That... was cool!" I think it was the first time she had ever played a piece without breaking down. She was on fire. The recital was a success, her parents were overjoyed and astonished and she continued to progress, at times falling back to old habits, but generally going forward.

A couple of things made Beena "turn around." One was my refusal to let her float. But that alone would not have been enough for the long haul. She began to play well, and this was thrilling to her. And, she sensed I was taking her seriously as a pianist, something no one had done, including herself. Later her father told me in incredulous tones that Beena "respected me." I knew this was because I respected her first.

❧ The Way It's Spozed To Be

In the great book *The Way It's Spozed To Be*, James Herndon recounts his experience teaching in what he termed a "deprived" school in the sixties. He was assigned the infamous 7H and 9D sections, the high schoolers who read on a first grade level if at all, wandered in and out of class and often rioted. Mr. Herndon decided not to do things the way they were spozed to be done, since they obviously weren't working. The way he was spozed to run the class was: pass out workbooks at the start of the period, collect them with no writing in them at the end, write checkmarks and low grades next to students' names, and wave them to the next level.

Instead, he loosened the reins and allowed a little chaos. Laughter, yelling, and name-calling took place, but along with it came a general sense that you could be at school and still be human.

He had them write their favorite songs on the board every day, the *top forty lists* as they called them. They would also have readings of elementary plays, with the few who could read sounding out words, usually producing *Cinderella* over and over again. He encouraged them to talk about things in their lives they cared about, and write small essays. When spring came and the annual school riots took place, his class was the only one that didn't participate. They were too interested in putting on *Cinderella* yet one more time, or discussing where they went on the bus over the weekend. Around the same time, one of the students, Harvey, suddenly discovered he could read:

> *Everybody clapped and cheered; naturally there were a few calls of ... chump mixed in. After the ovation Harvey couldn't shut up; he was in a daze. He kept talking like a reformed drunkard, telling about how bad things were when he couldn't read, how he knew all the letters, but put them together and they just didn't mean anything to him before, but now... and what he planned to read next...them comics...*

Progress was slow and by objective measure, Mr. Herndon had no control over his class. He was fired and told that he just didn't have it in him to be a teacher. Meanwhile, Harvey could read...

❧ Turnaround

I refuse to fill notebook after notebook with one-word assignments, listen with gritted teeth to unprepared performances and when the student finally changes teachers again, breathe a sigh of relief. If a student lacks the faith, confidence, or knowledge that he can be a fine musician, I refuse to be silent on the subject and thus reinforce his negative impression.

In all the diversity of my studio, it is important that students develop at least one quality in common. They must all believe that they can be star students, make beautiful sounds, acquire fluid techniques, and play with profound musical ideas. If I can convince students to think this way, after they have had other conceptions of themselves, I have succeeded in applying the only label I find acceptable, the *turnaround*.

TALENT

Talent is a word that tends to limit people in different ways.

But before I go on, let me say that talent, in the music field, is a very real quantity. It describes the ease and speed with which a student learns and progresses. It describes physical and aural skills and refers to the beauty and imagination in a musician's performance. But students who don't naturally display these gifts are often classified as *untalented* and are not given the same attention. Teacher expectations are down, and unimpressive results often follow.

Another word that limits us when discussing talent is the verb to have. We say that a student does not *have talent*, when perhaps she is simply not displaying it. Perhaps she has problems with coordination, body awareness, rhythmic sensitivity, interpersonal empathy, or focus. We say a student does not have talent when in fact her profound feel for music is simply blocked by physical and spiritual obstacles.

On the other end of the spectrum, students who are considered talented, but have trouble producing up to their potential, are often stigmatized as lazy or difficult. Only the musical aspects of that person were considered and they were branded as super achievers, when in fact they might have problems in personality, character, mind or soul that are just as real and powerful as their obvious musical facility.

۞ Definition

The first problem is the narrow definition of talent. There are many strengths that can raise a so-called average student to an excellent level of performance.

In the narrow definition of musical talent, the average piano students' characteristics are easy to spot. They may have normal difficulties with technique, fairly responsive coordination, and not-so-accurate pitch recognition. But I look beyond these easy problems to spot unconventional talents.

- Bravery is probably one of the greatest talents. It carries students to great heights because it allows them to believe in their music and their taste, and to seek out criticism.
- Passion is a cousin to talent and can be harnessed to produce good results.
- A flexible, open mind allows a student to change habits and beliefs that limit him.

- Introspective, profound caste of thought lends itself to a thoughtful, sensitive interpretation.
- Spontaneity and ability to be in the moment makes the music seem alive.
- Imagination can help bring artistry and texture to a performance.
- An overriding joy in a student can bring a magical quality to her performance.
- Persistence, intelligence, and discipline are among the other key qualities demonstrated by students.

Even negativity that exists in a student's life can act as a talent of sorts, even though it can be painful:

- A melancholy streak can compel a student to "find relief" in musical experiments and can imbue performances with a sweet, dark quality.
- Even anger and jealousy can propel a student to learn an instrument well. Anger, especially, can inform performances with an extra edge.
- A dysfunctional home or community environment, if the student is strong, can act as impetus toward musical study, as escape, or as a way for the student to bring something good into his life. In the long run, of course, these and other negative qualities are useful only as motivators or material for artistic memory.

If I as a teacher can learn to perceive a student's personal qualities as musical talents, I can help him toward the goal of fine pianism.

By the same token, a student with traditional musical gifts may have blockages in his body, spirit, or personality that hinders obvious abilities. He may not possess the qualities listed above and may find it hard to express and fully develop musicality.

Comic book heroes all have special unique powers. Often these powers will be very specific. But there is always a time when their powers are not enough. Then they must use them in a creative manner to defeat the enemy.

I define the word talent to include all qualities necessary in a student's musical education, including physical, musical, psychological and spiritual aspects. And I like to reserve judgment on a student's musical potential until I understand what is getting in the way of his powers of clear and graceful expression.

NATIVE TONGUE FLUENCY

❧ Musical Skills as Language Skills, Some Native, Some Second Language

Talent that is specifically musical in nature, such as physical ease, a highly developed ear, and imaginative powers, are very real, as I mentioned before. As a music teacher, I have seen it often enough.

But again, I limit myself as a teacher when I assume that even these specific musical skills must be given at birth. Pitch recognition, for example, can be learned. I was born with naturally tin ears. But after years of singing every day, writing songs, and teaching solfege (do-re-mi), I have learned *relative pitch* and, on some days, can even muster an approximation of *perfect pitch,* or more precisely, *memorized pitch.*

It is interesting to examine musical skills in the same light as language skills. We grow up speaking one or more languages that then become our native tongue or tongues. We achieve native fluency in these languages. But it is possible later in life to develop native fluency in other spoken languages.

An ear receptive to pitch differences, body aware-ness that enables fluid technique, a sensitive nature that lets a student connect to her music, are all quali-ties that, when a student possesses them from birth, are called *talents*. It is helpful to also call them native languages. Like language skills, I can examine the com-ponents that make up specific musical skills. Then I can help students who were not born with them ac-quire them as a second language.

♪ Add to the Vocabulary

I do not want to make the irresponsible assertion that all musicians are equal in their potential for music making. But we all have a certain vocabulary of musical skills and facilities. It is important to realize that many of these can be learned.

A talent for naturally fluid technique, for example, can be perceived as not having many obstacles or knots. Students who weren't born with this fluidity must simply spend more time consciously removing knots. Then, a more natural technique can become part of their physical vocabulary.

With specific analysis of what the problems were, proper training, patience and faith, and a willingness to surrender spiritual and physical blockage, students can achieve fluency in most of the musical language skill sets.

WESTERN CLASSICAL MUSIC
AS LEARNED IDIOM

❧ All Musical Languages Have the Same Purpose

A student who grew up in a different culture and listened to music other than western music can still learn the logic and subtleties of western classical music. All world music, such as Indian Classical or Chinese Folk, has direct connections to Western classical music.

On a spiritual level, all world dramatical languages achieve the same purpose as western music. As in a spoken language, the purpose of all musical idioms is to describe, recreate, heighten and ennoble the human condition.

On a dramatic level, all music has as its goal to leave home, undertake some transformation, and return home.

❧ The Tonic, et al

As I write this, my family and I are walking through an Indian bazaar, with wild classical Indian music spinning around our heads. I notice the following.

This music has a *tonic*, a home to start from and return to, a tonal center around which the other tones are assembled: a goal. The tonic in world music idioms may not be the endpoint of a western major scale. It may be a pentatonic scale or other scale system. Perhaps the tonic is not even the first note of their scale, but it is home.

As I listen to these deliciously exotic sounds, as foreign, busy and chaotic as the market I am in, a note that serves as the tonic occurs again and again. Melodies whine and buzz around it, but always return to the *father tone*. The start and endpoint define the journey taken.

Also, these other music languages have *dominants*. The dominant in Chinese folk songs has the exact same pitch relation to the tonic as in western music, i.e., a perfect fifth. But in other music idioms, for example the music I am hearing now, the dominant may simply be the tone that tends to exert a strong or "dominant" pull toward the tonic.

Perhaps it could be called the *leading tone*. It doesn't matter. It need only be some note-exerting tension, pulling us back.

I am also hearing phrases and their endpoints, cadences, emerging.

In fact, many of the mechanics of western music can be found in world music. Inner logic, reasoning, pathways, pauses, hesitations, obstacles, detours, elaborations, working out, and resolutions are found in all systems and touch us on a human level, because they speak of the same events in our lives. I am borrowing from the beautiful writings of Heinrich Schenker. Although his system of theoretical analysis was designed especially for classical composers, such as Beethoven, his writing eloquently relates classical music to life and philosophy, and highlights the universal qualities of music in general.

Thus all students, whatever their native cultures may be, whatever their listening habits, can learn an affinity to western classical repertoire. All they need are musical skills and an ear for life.

THE CATERPILLAR'S SECOND SKIN: REMOVE BARRIERS BETWEEN TEACHER AND STUDENT

Caterpillars are as different as from each other as their adult forms are different from other adult forms. Some can be smooth and naked, while others have dense hairy coats of many different colors. Still others have spines or long whiskers.

> ～ Life Cycle of a Butterfly, Bellevue State Park Website
> http://www.state.ia.us/parks/lifecycl.htm

My first goal as teacher is to bring the student's mind and heart as close as possible to me and to the music.

Jimmy Mack's Barber Shop

§ Cherish the Humanity of Students for Maximum
   Communication

Jimmy Mack is a master communicator. He is also
the first barber to give me a human-looking haircut.
Part of it's the "coif," but it's also that he makes me
feel human when I'm there.

I have always seen barbershops as a bit dehumaniz-
ing. I climb into a chair, they hoist me above the crowd,
cover everything except my head, and then take scis-
sors to it. I am forced to look at myself in the mirror;
under the garish light every little flaw jumps out. In
the background you can see all the other "heads" looking at you. The barber talks to you, but it's usually
forced and he usually gets too personal too fast.

Not Jimmy. First of all, the chair faces away from
the mirror, toward the small group of men always assembled there. Jimmy knows I don't want to be shown
the back of my head when it's done, I don't want to see
it at all. I trust him, and he trusts me to trust him.

Secondly, if we do talk, it's about real things. He might tell about the previous owner of my house, across the street from the shop. And if he senses I want to be silent, he doesn't talk to me at all.

Then, there's an almost mystical way that he has of touching our heads. He's gentle, not pulling you around like a piece of meat, like most barbers. And for some elderly men who come in with just a sprout or two of hair, he isn't really even giving a cut. He is massaging them, giving them succor. 'Round and 'round his buzzing razor goes on their scalps until they gaze out from the chair, hypnotized and peaceful.

❦ Succor

I aspire to Jimmy's sense of humanity in my teaching. If students cough, they get water. If they sneeze or cry, they get tissue. If they are tired or sad, I might play for them.

And I remind myself that there are some students with "just a sprout or two of hair." I am not referring to amount of talent, but rather their motivation for studying. It might not be immediately apparent to me what they get out of it, but I have faith that they are happy with whatever that is.

They don't have to be bubbling over with talk or smiles, or constantly reassuring me how much they love piano. I only require that they want to be there and that they go about becoming the finest musician they can be. Meanwhile I can massage their "musical scalps" and perhaps help them, like the men at Jimmy's Barber Shop, find succor.

Student as Education Expert

❧ Active and Passive Roles

The words *teach* and *learn* trouble me a bit. They imply that the instructor is only active and the student is only passive.

Teaching is often based on this model. The student goes into a classroom or lesson, opens his beak and the teacher pours in the worms. These roles are reinforced everywhere in the classroom. The teacher has a big desk, in front of the room. The teacher is the adult, the teacher is the authority figure, the disciplinarian, the expert. The teacher runs the classes every time. The teacher judges the student, rarely vice versa. The teacher talks, the student listens. The student must raise his hand, the teacher doesn't need to. The teacher gets to be creative and proactive, the student is for the most part required to be reactive.

In short, the very skills that are necessary to become creative and innovative members of a democratic and free market society are not given the student in school.

I'm not advocating the removal of the teacher's authority. Yes, someone has to run the lessons and classes, just as a manager has to run a business meeting. But as a teacher, I must be careful not to let the icons of authority overwhelm the student and paralyze him. Instead, the messages we give students must also confirm the active role of the student.

Most importantly, I must not withhold essential life skills, such as independent thinking and inference, from the student, in the name of my own authority.

❧ Analogy to Health Profession

An analogy to the teacher/student relationship is healer and patient. This is a good example because western medicine has tended to downplay the patient's role in healing. Pills are prescribed, tests are done, and prognoses are given, with or without explanation. The patient and his own healing power are ignored.

A medical doctor recently told me that holistic remedies often don't achieve results. But Dr. Mehl-Madrona, in *Coyote Medicine*, explains that holistic remedies often fail because they require active participation of the patient.

Native American shamans spend a few days with a patient. They ask about the family, sometimes meet the family, and ask about the patient's spiritual beliefs, emotional state, and lifestyle. The whole person and her soul are considered. And the patient takes an active role in healing. Shamans consider themselves responsible for only a small portion of the cure. Although the shaman is called a *healer*, the patient is also actively *healing* himself.

❧ New Words for Teach and Learn

I suggest we come up with a new word that means both "teach" and "learn," analogous to the two-sided word "heal." Something like the word "seek." Then the tutor and pupil are both seeking. Or what about these words:

- ❧ reflect
- ❧ discover
- ❧ uncover
- ❧ acknowledge
- ❧ commune
- ❧ exchange
- ❧ build

We could also make up a new word for the overall teaching/learning process:

- ❧ Archeosyn
- ❧ Synarchate
- ❧ Synarch

These three come from the two words "archeology" and "synthesis," where on the one hand we are all digging, but we are sharing the burden.

Then, I think students need to be invited/encouraged/required to participate, from the earliest grades onward. In piano lessons, I like to ask a student a lot of questions.

- ☙ Did the work we just did on a piece help them understand and practice it better?
- ☙ Is there anything else with which they need help?

☙ Student as Education Expert...

Asking about the work we do together has a double benefit. First, it conveys to them the idea that they are part of the teaching process. They have a say in whether I am giving the right advice, whether it works for them. Of course I will know if my advice works if they can solve the problem in question, but asking them for their thoughts lets them know they are also expected to think about the problem and the best way to solve it.

Secondly, by asking them if my suggestion "worked for them," I am opening up a whole new resource often not tapped into: the student herself. So often we go to the parents, books or seminars as resources for learning about the student, but so seldom do we actually ask her. The assumption is that she doesn't know what she needs. But this is wrong.

We have all "gone back to school" as adults, either in conferences, private lessons, continuing education courses or even just self-study. I have done my best learning as an adult. I have been a very involved and thinking participant in my education. As a piano student, I ask myriad questions and express my own ideas. Sometimes I have reverted, in an educational setting, to a child's mentality: "Don't ask questions, just listen." But then I remember that, although my "stupid" idea or thought might be wrong, wrong, wrong, it might open the door to either the right answer or an original idea. Then I am never afraid to ask.

When I was in high school physics class, one homework problem required the time of the earth spinning on its rotation. I raised my hand and asked, "What should we use as "T," the time for rotation?" Everybody in the class turned and gave me a scowl. Of course it's twenty-four hours, you moron, was written on their faces. But later I found out that the time of rotation actually varies, albeit slightly. I would never have discovered this if I had been afraid to question conventional wisdom. But this kind of open questioning on my part was rare when I was young.

I love asking students questions out of the blue, unexpectedly making them partners in their own tutelage. Funny, though, they never look surprised! Adults might think it's unusual to ask them what they think about educational methods, but students think it's normal! They answer me as if they were just waiting for me to ask.

Other questions I ask students are the following:

- ❧ Can they think of how to solve a certain problem?
- ❧ What do they think needs addressing in their playing?
- ❧ How did they like the piece I just played for them?

Now it's their turn. In addition to critiquing my problem-solving, they have to analyze and come up with solutions on their own initiative.

I think students are experts on education. After all, for the first twenty-two years of their lives, it is their primary job! Yet we rarely go to them for advice on the subject!

❧ Approximation

One of my biggest challenges is to know exactly what to teach in any given lesson. Sure, I do lesson plans and have general goals for students, and know what I need to say after they play a piece or exercise. But so many young students, and some adults, present a blank face at lessons. They are nervous and humble and expect me to know everything and give them exactly what they need. But my words are only approximate, my truths only partial. No matter how objective and expert I become, I will only be taking an average of what the student needs.

I say that because I have my own perspective on how to approach a problem. Perhaps I think it is a technical issue. Another teacher might think if you just concentrate on sound, the technique will take care of itself. Someone else might think the interpretation is not focused and that will fix things.

But what does the student think? She is there all week. Is the problem the sound? Are your ideas for the piece clear enough? Or is it that your thumb is simply slipping off the keys? If I invite the student to verbalize what is happening, they make my job much more exact.

Again, a shaman asks the patient what is wrong, even though the healer may have an idea already. This is because the patient knows better than anyone about his own body, life experiences, soul and other factors that may have led to the condition.

⸙ Participatory Education leads to Proactive Life

The more I can involve a student in his own education, and invite him to think and discover along with me, the more he will retain and the more he will want to learn. True curiosity and discovery of meaning are infectious, and will lead to a lifetime of creativity and new ideas.

But as long as there are strict lines between teaching and learning, students will depend on teachers for answers and worse: for the questions. Students who are forced to take a passive role later replace teachers with television sets. Rather than do their own thinking, they rely on ministers, priests, and politicians. Ethics are managed by accountants and lawyers who advise not on what is right, but how far we can go and still get away with it.

I believe passivity in education is to a large degree responsible for the abdication of accountability in many sectors of our society. If an active role in our own thinking is taught from an early age, it will be up to us to find our own faith and redemption, in the polling booths and town halls, in our businesses and homes, and in our own souls.

Active Love

✦ Planting Faith in the Student's Soul

We all know what it means to truly love, to be in love. With a lover, or a friend, or a student.

When we love someone with our entire soul, there is so much that is activated within us. With a beloved student, for example, we can forgive mistakes, not practicing, flakiness or temper. It's all easy, because in the end, our abiding affection enables us to see past her temporary madness and infidelity to her work.

It is this ability to see past the occasional loss of footing in a student that enables him to continue to progress and to maintain his faith, because my love is a kind of active faith. I extend to him the notion that he should continue, that it's okay to "fall down."

Therefore, love of this profound kind is important because it enables me to be very near the soul of this student and to plant in it the fire of faith. Like Prometheus giving the gift of fire to mortals, we are able to love the student so much we can sacrifice a bit of our sanity for him.

✎ Active Love for All

When we have experienced this total nurturing love for one student, we can learn from our actions toward that student and from our reactions to her and her misdeeds. Our experience can then be a teacher, a model, for how we can act toward and react to all students.

This way of extending love to all students, based on our past experience in love, I call *active love*.

There is a saying: "Love is a decision." This is true for one person, and it is especially true for many.

If we practice *active love* often and gracefully enough, we will succeed in planting a strong faith and confidence in our students. They will grow and their power will double, because our souls and theirs are joined.

LISTENING TO THE STUDENT'S SOUL

I've heard such unearthly, unnamed music in my dreams. It is so distinct, so lovely. It seems endless, and I can just listen. I wish I could remember it!

This is my connection to the infinite, to the Divine, I believe. It is very deeply buried, surrounded like a pristine, secret garden by the dark forest of my imperfect waking thoughts.

Sometimes small creative urges appear during the day, incomplete and awkward. They are tiny glimpses of the infinite, revealing themselves during daylight hours. So often they show themselves as mistakes or ideas so different from our normal conscious ones that we quickly cover them. They appear to be little aliens, wandering around in our world. So we hide them.

Perhaps it is half of an idea on how to interpret a piece. Perhaps it is half a melody. Perhaps it is half of a realization about the cause of a particular student's problem. The form that it takes when it comes to us appears to be wrong. As it is, it gives no solution.

I put it away for a while if it doesn't make any sense yet. Someday it may come to full flower, maybe in a few days, maybe a few years.

If we listen to these blips and have faith in them, they can eventually grow into a wonderful reality. The skill of listening to these small baubles and burps, these soul mutterings, has become a sort of teaching philosophy for me. In this way, I can cherish and nurture the incipient signs of creation in my students and those around me.

♪ Soul Mutterings of the Student

Students often fiddle and noodle at the piano, especially before the lesson. Sometimes this is just nervous energy, but at times it has the makings of a composition. Even accidentally, they will hit on a frenetic scale pattern they like and sequence it up, one step at a time.

Or they "get stuck" on a short chord progression that they stumbled onto, pedaling and making a contemplative sound portrait.

I always ask them if they "made it up," If we have time, I'll help them write it down.

Sometimes I hear two or three notes together that make a unique melodic fragment that they haven't noticed. They have left it behind and are noodling onward. I will try to recreate it and write it down for them.

Sometimes I will simply leave it at that, entering it in the log of student composition. Seeing their piece written on a real staff with the date and their name next to it is always gratifying for them. I've had some prolific composers with over twenty entries in the log.

Some pieces warrant a fleshing out, and they will play them at recital.

Having their creations recorded heightens their confidence. Also, when playing their own pieces they begin to think like a composer. This musical thinking carries over to their repertoire.

Most importantly, it impresses on the students the importance of listening more closely to their accidents, to their warm-ups, to their own and others' music. Listening to their own and to others' souls.

The Mistake as Guide

❧ What is a Mistake?

Another name for a mistake is a *unique idea in its infancy*. Although most mistakes should be corrected, still they show the true face of the individual making them. As a teacher, I gain insight into students' minds and personalities through their mistakes. And sometimes mistakes are little spitting sparks of inspiration, ugly enough now, but waiting to be recognized. Then they can be fanned with the breezes of taste and judgment to become beautiful artistic flames.

❧ We Hide Our Flaws

People are a big mystery. The face we present on any given day is a portrait of everything that has ever happened to us, and our inherited genetics and traditions. So of course it is impossible to read. There is too much there.

We tend to hide our "spiritual face," to not give away clues. Why would we want to tell everyone our life story?

Students are even more guarded, and I include myself when I am taking a lesson or class. I don't want to show my flaws, so I keep a calm face and play the way that I think the teacher will accept, and carry myself *professionally*. In short, I hide.

I don't show myself. For better or worse, much of my individuality is hidden. The result is, my true creativity is never developed. No one, including myself, hears my *unique ideas in their infancy*, and then what is developed is a correct, clean, but faceless artistry. It is what Russell Sherman, author of the book *Piano Pieces*, refers to as musical in the conventional sense, but boring and missing the spark of originality.

֍ Mistake as Guide

Therefore, because there is so much mystery and guardedness in my students, I cherish their mistakes. I seek guidance from them. They are clues to what my student is really thinking and how they approach music. The following are examples of some of these clues.

֍ Mistakes That Reveal Personality

Recently a girl of about seven was playing one of her first staff pieces, Faber and Faber's *Best Friends*, from the *Piano Adventures* series. It was the first example of both hands playing at the same time, a major development for a young pianist. The right hand played a quarter note at the same time as the left hand, so the whole chord was to last one beat.

But my student was holding it longer, even after I pointed out that it was one beat. I noticed she was pushing down on the keys fiercely, almost hanging on them. I asked her why.

"Because I'm confused," she said with a bewildered scowl.

"I see, so really pushing the keys makes you feel safer?" I asked, to which she said "yes."

Playing both hands at the same time made her feel a bit lost, so she dug in, and of course the rhythm was off. This was a wonderful window into her personality and reaction pattern. Now I can use this insight in other contexts and maybe even help her to be more confident over time.

Another student, a teenage boy, was playing triads and inversions, and notes within each chord were not sounding simultaneously. I was getting ready to give advice on playing notes at the same time, when I noticed he wasn't really lining up the fingers on the right notes before playing.

Although he is calm and always smiling, this mistake reminds me that he is a teenager and full of impatience and random energy. So to blow off steam, we worked on using arm weight and the upper body to make fortissimos in his triads. After giving off some energy, he was more able to focus and aim his hands before playing the chords. He beamed to hear this new sound, perfectly simultaneous, deep and gloriously loud!

At times a student wants to make a ritardando or accelerando, but won't tell me. I wonder how many times I've corrected rhythm without first asking, "Is that what you wanted to do?" How many incipient efforts at interpretation have been in vain, silenced by my relentless drive for smooth, faceless, error-free playing!

Yes, the ritardando might be too clumsy or the accelerando too rash, but the impulse is there, and taste must be learned. Therefore, I try to ask as often as possible, what the student's intention is. Then we can work on refining it.

One beginner was playing C up to G when it was written C-C-G. I showed her the extra note but she just wasn't seeing it. Then I realized the lyrics to the simple song were "C and G," written under the notes C-C-G. She was so affected by the words that she literally couldn't see the extra note, even when I pointed it out several times.

If I only see that she is not focusing on the staff, I would miss a more important trait, her awareness and sensitivity. I had sensed she was very emotional and intuitive at our first interview. I had told her to please sit on the sofa, not the piano bench, and that she could play later. She started to cry and her big, dark eyes at that moment held all the sentiment required for a Chopin mazurka. Of course I accepted her!

One nine-year-old student likes to improvise dreamy compositions whenever I am writing in her notebook or before a lesson. In one of her pieces, the last four notes in the left hand are *D-C-B*, descending to tonic *G*. She couldn't stop herself from playing *D-C-B-A-G*, all five notes in the G position. I couldn't figure out why, until I realized, that she was filling in the *A* to smooth out the bass line. I asked her if she thought it sounded better her way, and she said it did.

I was reminded that she is always listening to her music with a composer's ear, and is very aware of the beauty of the melodic line. This is of course a treasure for a student to have. Her mistake revealed to me her deep appreciation for the phrase, and I can focus on this aspect more than with other beginning students.

Galina Prilutskiy, a respected piano pedagogue who teaches at the Westminster Conservatory in Princeton, New Jersey, is the very model of a nurturing teacher. I'll always remember her comment about a student who tended to rush: "It shows that she is has so much to say that she's trying to get it out all at once!" What a wonderful way of looking at it. And true.

Mistakes can be windows into our students' souls. They are the part of the student that is unique. Instead of immediately jumping on an error, I try to see if it can help me get closer to the student as a result of understanding it.

Our Sacred Objects
and Ceremonies

Teaching is an indirect art, a coaxing, suggestive process, like any leadership or mentoring position. Because we do not have direct control over the actions of our students, we have to rely on example, persuasion and the various wonderful, unspoken *tricks* we have gathered, basket by basketful, in the mysterious foggy fields of experience.

Some *tricks* are not even known to us, just mannerisms, maybe the way we hold our bodies or our facial expressions, or a certain inflection in the voice, that gets the desired reaction. Perhaps it is a way of dressing or talking to the parents. Perhaps it is the rapport we develop with the students. Or the way the studio smells when they enter for a lesson.

These are our tools. Shamans, indigenous healers, must also rely on subtle powers of suggestion to achieve their results. They literally keep a bag of *tricks*, but they call them *sacred objects*. The sacred objects might include a feather from a particular bird, a whisker from a cheetah, a rock, or a crystal.

They also rely on rituals and ceremony to help the patient heal. They might pour water over hot stones, have the patient smoke or imbibe certain substances in order to shift consciousness, make prayer flags, and perform rituals outdoors at different times of day and night. All of these actions and settings have an intended effect on the patient.

◈ Our Sacred Objects and Ceremonies

Just as a shaman carefully collects sacred objects through his career and puts them in a special bag, I have found it useful to keep my own *sacred objects*. I keep those that seem to work and discard others.

Although we may not take steps that are specifically designed as ceremonies, I believe a lot of the things we do in the presence of students have ceremonial effect.

Among the powerful sacred objects are wardrobe and appearance. When I started teaching, I often wore jeans and polo shirts, or dress shirts not tucked in. I wore my hair long and unkempt, and alternated between long and one-day beards, goatees, and mustaches. My style of dress was intended as a sacred object or a ritual in my teaching. My intended effect was for the students to feel comfortable and also to open them up to alternative ways of being, opening creative thought.

I found, however, that this particular ritual was not serving its purpose. For one thing, I had moved from New York City, where this was acceptable, to an affluent suburb with a conservative lifestyle. Although students and parents connected to me and recognized my *bohemian look* as a creative trademark, I felt more and more that students were not taking me as seriously. I had motivational and at times disciplinary problems with them. I realized that they were a bit too comfortable. I finally had an awakening when a young student said, "Did you go to music school or are you just a guy in the neighborhood who likes to have fun with kids?"

I decided to have a *makeover.* Over the period of about a year, I shaved my beard and mustache, found Jimmy Mack, and located some dress shirts, slacks, nice shoes and ties that I could tolerate and also afford. I made sure to wear these at every lesson. I got a lot of teasing from parents and students when it first happened ("Hey look, Mr. D. is all grown up!"). But I believe it has had a sobering effect on my students, especially new ones.

It's not that shirts and ties are the only answer for these children. My students are varied and international. They see and wear all kinds of dress, from traditional Chinese and Korean, to Indian Saris, to Japanese kimonos, to inner-city hip-hop. But I think that people in this kind of community have certain subconscious associations with conservative, professional attire. A tie is the sacred object of this social sector. If I lived in the Outback and were teaching invisibility, a shirt and tie would have a negative impact on my credibility. There, I would be taken more seriously in a simple cloth or even naked.

❧ Reputation and Image as Sacred Objects

Different teachers rely on different sacred objects and rituals. I know a teacher who wears jeans and tee shirts, while living in a similar community to mine. She relies on another sacred object: her image as folk artist and composer. Because of her big name in folk music, her casual dress is actually a badge of honor, and holds its own power for students. She stands out and commands respect for her boldness and creativity.

I know a few teachers who have international concert careers, and national reputations as teachers. They hold a sacred object in their renown. I have seen students transfer to their studios and drop habits that previous teachers were standing on their head to make them drop. I don't believe it was only the gifts and skills of the more famous pedagogue that *did the trick.*

I think the teacher's fame as a pedagogue alone is often a key factor in a student's transformation. Students decide to practice, they decide to listen, they decide to examine their playing, because the person speaking to them is famous, even though the previous teacher might have asked for the same changes, in much the same way. The fame, the name, the face seen on CD covers and in seminars, those are the sacred objects.

How does this help those of us who don't enjoy international reputations? I think we can learn from the power of reputation, and use it to maximum advantage. We can build up credibility in our community.

But more importantly, we can learn from famous pedagogues the power of image. Then we can modify our own for maximum influence.

❧ Everyday Tasks as Rituals

Shamans such as Dr. Mehl-Madrona and others have made me aware that even simple actions hold far more than their literal value. And I can use this to my advantage.

For example, I like to write notes on each lesson, and file them in a binder. In addition to the literal benefit of tracking and planning lessons, I believe that the moments I spend writing have spiritual, ceremonial benefits during the lesson. First, it has a soothing effect; it is a moment of silence for the students. They get relief from their efforts, and can contemplate what we just did. They also see me writing very solemnly on a sheet of lined paper that will go into a huge binder. It looks professional, it appears that I am taking the lesson seriously enough to record certain parts of it in writing, and that I am taking the students seriously. Occasionally I will get jokes from older students: "Oh, you're taking notes on me!" But I think they do appreciate this level of healthy attention.

Another example is playing for students. Often I will sit next to the student and lean over to play a passage or scale. But if I want to emphasize a particular demonstration, play a new piece or show a new technique, I will ask them, "May I play for you?" I let them come out the side nearest other chair, while I go around the other way. I sit for a few seconds, sometimes even closing my eyes first. When finished, I ask them how they enjoyed it, or whether they understand.

In other words, I *underline* the moment, and they will remember it more clearly. I show them respect and they are more willing to respect the music.

❧ Some Pedagogues and Their Sacred Powers

Galina Prilutskiy once told me: "When I touch a student's hand, it helps me and helps them. It relaxes them." If you knew Galina, you would understand; she is very gentle and has a soft voice that lilts upward in a soothing way. She has wonderful, frizzy red hair and a sensitive, understanding smile with eyes that are artistic and both twinkling and slightly melancholy. All these qualities act as her sacred objects; they bring peace and empathy to her students, who have won many major competitions. For her, even just smiling at a student has magical, ceremonial effect, not to mention touching his hand.

I saw Marvin Blickenstaff, the editor, composer and piano clinician, speak at a seminar. He has a soothing, resonant voice, with a timbre and range somewhere between a bassoon and a cello. This wonderful voice echoed in the lecture hall and filled about fifty piano teachers with warmth. You could see it in our faces — we looked like happy children, staring up at him, smiling and nodding.

I can imagine that a student in his studio feels the same nurturing energy. In addition, he has very expressive hand and face gestures that punctuate his words, and rhythmic way of pacing in front of us that was very hypnotic and soothing.

James Goldsworthy, recording artist, music historian, and associate dean of the Westminster Choir College, has an excited, animated energy when giving talks on history. He makes intellectual discoveries that shed unique new light on old forms, like a talk he gave on Beethoven scherzos. He played part of a symphony and was literally dancing around the podium. After the talk I approached him and he grabbed my hand, smiling and excitedly continuing to make various points. In other words, his enthusiastic energy invited me to explore these new ideas, to be joyful, to get worked up, and I did!

All successful teachers have manners that act as sacred objects on their students or listeners. We all have our own ways of acting — mannerisms, facial expressions and vocal tones that work.

❧ Finding Our Sacred Objects and Rituals

I don't mean false mannerisms. This is just manipulation, in effect a lie. Students can always smell lies and thus falseness won't convince.

It's simple to find your own true, natural sacred objects and rituals. I notice how I act when I feel most natural and when I am excited by my work, and I notice when the student's face is the most engaged. Then I remember what objects or ceremonies were engaging us at the time.

The student doesn't have to be laughing, or smiling, or anything in particular. But there is a glow of recognition when we make this connection. If we are observant, we can use a concrete object or action to recapture that connection at a later time.

WORDS AS SACRED OBJECTS

Just as our actions, manner and dress act as sacred objects in our teaching, so do words. They are perhaps the most common and powerful of our sacred objects.

❧ Words as Madness

Words are more than information. Words are more than art, politics or spirituality. Words, at their very essence, are a subtle form of madness, an unreality that we have introduced to the primordial human condition. Even the simplest statement, such as "I am hungry," is unreal and unnatural. Describing reality demonstrates that, in fact, we are able to describe reality, in itself strange. To make a comment on life is adding to life, changing it.

Language, as practiced by most humans, adds new meaning to the world. At worst, it is falseness and manipulation, at best, an empowering force. Just the *fact* of words can alter consciousness.

Therefore, if I want to reach others with words, I must always remember to listen to the heart, others' and mine. Words must be carefully chosen to reflect what I hear.

If I want to use words to change my heart or others', I must choose words that will create a spiritually healthy reality, and then our hearts will listen to it.

◈ Words as Barriers

They can be my downfall, when I use too many. People are talked to all day. We are told things by other teachers, salesmen, radio and television talking heads, our friends, and our family. Thus words can be associated with authority, or stress, or simply too much sound. If I am not careful, simply the fact that I am talking to the student might overwhelm him.

Also, my words might be chosen wrongly. They might be too colorful and interesting, when simply telling him to count will do. Or, my mundane instructions may not help him interpret a piece; then I can call on more imaginative words to help the student *connect*.

◈ Silence

Silence is an important part of teaching. If I ask a student a question, and then remain silent for a while, she will trust that I sincerely want to hear her thoughts.

If I ask her if I have helped her, that is a difficult question for a student to answer. It means she might have to criticize her teacher and say, "no." Silence will give her the right words and also the bravery to do so.

If I ask what is wrong with her piece, she needs to hear it in her head, or concentrate on what happened during the week.

If I ask her if she likes a piece I just played, she needs to listen to the music still floating in the air and in her heart.

And if she is trying to get close to the music before starting to play it, I must give her silence.

ꝶ Our Most Powerful Sacred Object

Words can also be my most powerful sacred objects. They are certainly the ones most commonly used.

A different wording can help a student understand a concept that he never had before. The psychological aspect of words is as important as the meaning.

For example, I might tell a student to *sit up straight*. He might resist this, associating it with youth. If I say sit up *tall*, he might feel proud of his posture.

If I say, "Make a *ritardando* in that measure," he might hear it as another instruction, like "wipe your feet" or "please us a #2 pencil." Instead, I can say that this measure is the main character saying farewell, and leaving a loved one for a long time, so the student might feel a connection to this experience. Then he will want to say goodbye with a *ritardando*.

♄ Delivery

Of course the way I say a word might reinforce or contradict its meaning. Amy Greer, piano department head at Powers Music School in Belmont, Massachusetts, told me of how she found herself yelling at a student, "Play softly!" As she explained to me, "Yeah, that's really going to help!"

♄ Sensory Helper Words

Words can also be used to evoke sensorial reactions in the student. The most obvious is visual. But words describing the other senses can also be helpful.

A beautiful and lucid example of helpful imagery came from Adelaide B. McKelway, a private piano instructor in Virginia, formerly of Davidson College in North Carolina. She said:

> Regarding works such as Brahms, Op.118 No.2, or other works with a soprano melody, a deep and defining bass line, and more rapidly moving melodic material in a middle voice, students (envision) the ocean, the soprano line as an object floating on the surface, the middle voice as fish swimming beneath the surface, and the bass as an object touching the ocean floor.

This wonderful example uses all five senses! And it contains within it explanations for touch, balance, counterpoint and also mood!

≶ Student as Author

I learned from Jean Stackhouse, former head of the New England Conservatory Pre-College Division, that students write stories and poetry to better understand their pieces.

I asked a student to write a story using her favorite cartoon character to describe a minuet by Mozart. She had been playing correctly, but mechanically. Writing the story made her feel part of the process, responsible for the performance. Her playing became very personal and thoughtful and she later won a competition with this piece.

Another student, playing an arrangement of *The Swan*, wrote a story in which a swan was shot. He drew a picture of a gun and a bleeding swan. We had discussed the B section as a bit *troubled*, that maybe *something was wrong*. He was able to bring this out in his playing and connect to the piece on a deep level.

≶ Analogies

An analogy can be effective tool to solve technical or musical problems. One adult student of mine was playing her thumbs too loudly in Faber and Faber's great little gem, The *Rain Forest*. I asked her to play with smooth thumbs, but that's like saying: *Relax!* to somebody.

We stopped and built an image of a rain forest. It was dusk, just after a rain, the forest creatures were still. She closed her eyes, and after a few moments, played perfectly evenly.

One ten-year-old girl had trouble playing the last note of a piece more softly than the preceding note. I kept asking her to "taper off," but these words did not do it for her.

Finally I said, "Pretend the entire composition consists of only these two notes. You need to make an impression by playing the second one more softly." After pausing to consider this, she did a perfect diminuendo on the last note.

❧ The Thesaurus of Sensory Words and Analogies

There is a growing list of sensory helper words, images and analogies at releasethebutterfly.com. Please feel free to add your favorites.

❧ Students and Words

Although music ultimately has its own psychological and emotional world, accessed directly by the fingers, musical mind and heart, words provide another avenue to this world.

I allow for the power of words in my teaching, and invite the student to do the same. They are sacred objects that we can use to get closer and closer to the student and the music.

THE INNER ADULT

In psychology there is the phrase *inner child,* referring to the part of adults that needs nurturing and perhaps some maturing. I like to think about the *inner adult* in a child. That is not to say they need to give up childlike qualities, such as wonder and enthusiasm.

More than anything, I think children love to do *real-life* things. They long to make things and achieve. Why do small children play with trucks and play *house*? Enact battles with soldiers, drive cars on small plastic tracks and scoop sand with small bulldozers? Yes, it's imagination building, but it's also an act of empowerment. As a human being in training, a child lacks the essential ingredients for human happiness: power and freedom. The power to go places, to do things and to make their own decisions. Play, often seen as childish, is nevertheless a child's bid for freedom and strength. It is practice for adulthood, an opportunity to explore one's own capacities.

Even when children read books on fantasy they are engaged in the act of building, in this case an entire universe. And these stories often feature children as the protagonists, saving this or defeating that.

Even when an adult plays games, he is not being childish, but rather exploring a new area in *which he is not yet skilled. He is training a new inner adult.*

⚘ Fire Their Imagination with Their Own Capacities

I personally think games in lessons are a bit over-rated. They're useful as sugar coating for the absolute drudgework: learning finger numbers, note identification, et al. And they can fire the imagination and reinforce "data input." But even note identification, rhythm exercises, interval recognition, ear training, etc., if presented accurately and with meaning, can be thrilling for the youngest child.

- ❧ If you teach a new rhythm and they can directly apply it to sightreading or learning a piece, that's exciting.
- ❧ If they can name all the landmarks you ask them, and they couldn't do it the week before, that's exciting.
- ❧ If they can sight-read a short piece with two hands at once when for a long time they could only play a melody, that's exciting.

> ❖ And rewarding. And a child will take the meat
> and vegetable satisfaction over the sugar high of
> a game any day.

I like to make a *game* out of accomplishment and the acquisition of new abilities. If I approach everything with good humor and enthusiasm myself, the student will see all learning as a game.

❧ Students Respect Teachers Who Respect Their Ability to Achieve

When I was growing up, my mother was a writer and my father a businessman, so I was reading books and doing math problems at age four. As a result, the first five or six grades in school were essentially a walk through, usually with straight A's, about which I did not really care since I never had to work or think.

The first teacher, however, for whom I had to think and work, and not surprisingly for whom I developed a bit of an infatuation, was Miss True, my 7th grade biology teacher. She respected our intellect and work ethic. She went through all the species and phylums, from mitochondria to monkeys to man, and all the fascinating diagrams and Latin names in between. I drank it in, starved for such a banquet of information. I think it's true that even elementary students will respect a teacher who makes the class rigorous.

I went to school in the seventies, when teachers were trying to connect more on a psychological and social level. I'm all for that, when it's achieved subtly and efficiently. But it was too overt and too time- consuming.

I remember teachers who discussed social issues in lieu of entire lessons, or spent too much time with *psych* games like role-playing or sociological experiments in which we were the unwitting subjects. I didn't warm up to their classes, the material or the teachers. I was not sold because they did not bother really trying to sell the real thing: rigorous scholarship, and yes that exists at every level, from kindergarten through graduate school. It simply means your brain is engaged full tilt.

I've challenged myself, therefore, always to respect the student's love of rigor and achievement in lessons and the classroom. Because the most exciting thing for a human being, no matter what age, is to explore the heights and depths of his own potential.

ADDRESSING THE INNER ADULT

The essence of all cogent and important ideas is already contained within us at birth.

                  ~ Author

❧ Meaning as Power

The twin sister to achievement for children and students is meaning. Achievement represents power and freedom in a child's world and meaning represents understanding, another kind of power. To understand is to be included, and to have some control over outcome. For example, if I constantly tell a child to "sit up straight" or "sit tall," he will undoubtedly do it. But eventually he might slouch again. He will forget my advice or, if I am annoying enough that day, rebel against it. But if I point out that by sitting up, the student will correct his hand position and will improve on a piece he desperately wants to play, he might remember to sit up.

♬ Nonsense meters

Children have the best nonsense meters around. Classroom teaching is useful for understanding this like nothing else. There has never been a stand-up comedian, no matter how inexperienced or how tough the club, who has suffered the slings and arrows that a classroom teacher has if a class decides to sling. If you are not prepared, in any way, for them or for the material, they will let you know. On the other hand, there is nothing that will rivet a young person's attention like a sensible explanation of what was previously a mystery. And then you've got the audience in your pocket (and you're in theirs!).

♬ I reserve the right to understand

In a world of specialization, we as adults tend to surrender our right to understand the world around us. We might say:

- ‣ Singing and dancing are for the superstars and I'll gladly watch.
- ‣ There are financial experts who understand the market better than I ever will, so I won't plan for retirement.
- ‣ The minister or priest or rabbi is the one who reads the scriptures, why should I bother questioning my own faith?

↩ The doctor has about fifteen certificates on his
wall, so who am I to argue when he says the only
treatment for my disorder is medication that will
make me nauseated and possibly psychotic?

Children aren't yet ready for this cynicism. They
still believe they can understand the world, and why
not? They haven't yet been intimidated by experts.
And they are so right.

Very few complex concepts, if explained simply,
cannot be understood by most adults and most children. George Orwell said that if an idea was not strong
enough to be explained with short words, it was not a
strong idea.

❧ Trust that they will understand

I taught music history for six years to classes of
gifted young musicians. Many of them thought music
history would be the class they would have to suffer
through in order to get to chamber music and solo recitals, and for many, that idea never changed.

But a few golden groups and I went to the moon every week. Wheeee!!!! I made the decision at one point
to not gloss over musical concepts for a younger audience. And I mean young- many students were nine and
ten. I loved the challenge of taking a sophisticated

concept and (without oversimplifying it) presenting it to younger students.

So, subjects like Beethoven's *Heiligstadt Testament* being a possible suicide note, Schumann's last days in the asylum, Mozart's emotional insecurities and his desperate desire to please his oppressive father were all discussed. Without putting composers on the couch (too much) we were able to connect to them as people. What child hasn't felt oppressed by her parents or felt desperately alone or crazy? We didn't discount these masters' achievements by making them more mortal. On the contrary, we were able to get closer to their divine genius and bring more sensitivity into our performances of their music.

Even more academic concepts like changes in historical period were discussed in light of life experience and concepts they understood. For example, the Reformation was brought on by priests who just *weren't behaving.* The Counterreformation was enacted by the Catholic Church to call back the disillusioned flock. Thus, Vivaldi, the Red Priest, and other church composers, were called upon to write flashier, more sensational music as a musical attraction. Having laid the conceptual groundwork, we were able to listen to and study scores, and discuss specific aspects of Baroque virtuosity that might otherwise have been a dry exercise with no real historical underpinning.

In another example, I told them that J.S. Bach's children called him the *old peruke* (meaning stolid, archaic) and that they rebelled against his contrapuntal, involved Baroque style. They preferred to compose more freely, with chords in left hand and singing melody in the right. This style would introduce the Classical era.

We role-played in class, some students taking the part of C.P.E., the son, and some the part of J.S., the father. We played Baroque and Classical period pieces as a kind of debate. We didn't spend too much time on this, but were able to go from there to discussing specific aspects of counterpoint versus homophony, and the reaction of one historical period to another.

Lively discussions arose around these very true-to-life topics, every bit as sound and logical as ones in college music classes. Perhaps minus the intellectual jargon — but isn't that a plus?

One of my most inspiring teachers is actually my family physician, Dr. Timothy Sass at Princeton Internal Medicine Associates, P. C., because he explains medicine and physiology to me. By taking the time to explain my problems to me, he shows me respect and concern. He invites me to become involved and empowers me as a patient.

❧ Always Speak to the Inner Adult

I always want to texture concepts as much as possible.

If it is a sophisticated topic, such as interpretation or harmonic psychology, I must attempt to explain it at the student's level, wherever that is. Any concept can be explained to a person of any age. The essence of all cogent and important ideas is already contained within us from birth.

So, I just need a way to access the understanding that is already within the student. I need to connect the specific musical concept with the intuitive understanding of the world that they already hold.

If I always address the student's *inner adult,* he will be more involved, empowered and will develop independent thinking.

THE CATERPILLAR'S THIRD SKI
HELP REMOVE HABITS, VISIBLE
AND SPIRITUAL

The caterpillars are also vulnerable to predation by birds and other animals, which is why many of them have hairs, spines, or other defense mechanisms.

➤ Life Cycle of a Butterfly, Bellevue State Park Website
http://www.state.ia.us/parks/lifecycl.htm

Habits, patterns and ways of being that block progres
at the keyboard can be traced back to spiritual origins

When we are aware of these spiritual habits as p
nists, teachers and students, we can change, slowly
times, but inevitably.

Spiritual Habits

Once the communication is clear between teacher and student, all musical obstacles relate back to the spiritual state of the student.

The obstacle may manifest itself physically, as a mistake or habit. But the root is always within the student's personality and character.

Once I identify an obstacle, the student must first trust me, then we must agree on a solution. At that point the student must overcome the habit. If he does not, there is a spiritual reason.

❧ Examples of Habits and Their Spiritual Origins

Desire for Quick Results: If the student plays with frequent breakdowns, she doesn't practice well. This relates to a desire for easy gain and not understanding the rigors of mastery.

Flat Phrasing as a Result of Emotional and Verbal Flatness: If a student plays with flat phrasing, she is not interested in the emotional side of the piece, or she has difficulty accessing her own emotions.

If the former, the student might have arrogance or stubbornness, not wanting to admit that the emotions are part of it. He may shrug their shoulders and say, "I don't know!" often, rolling eyes. This might translate to "I don't care."

More often, though, the student is self-conscious about this emotion as a topic. He may be immature, young, or may simply have a stoic personality. He may be distant from his psychology, either by training or personality.

Often members of a student's family speak softly and with little inflection in their voices. They are calm and reasonable. The evenness and flatness in their vocal patterns will not help the student find inflection in his phrasing. And their reserved gestures and manner might make it harder for him to connect emotionally to his music. Of course this is not always true.

Lack of Physical Coordination and Some Causes: If a student plays with jellyfish fingers or faulty hand position, or slides all over the keys, he is not connected to his physical side.

Maybe the student does not engage in physical activities.

Perhaps the family members are reserved emotionally, or repressed. They might not be very tactile in showing affection, keeping hand-holding and other contact to a minimum. In this case, the student has not been taught that he has a body and how to be aware of it.

Perhaps the student was born with low coordination levels. Coordination and motor skills can be built up, through body awareness. But if peers and family taunt him, focusing on the image of physical difficulty, and not reinforcing the image of a future graceful human, the student will surrender his body awareness.

Perhaps the student has an active inner mind. A vivid imagination, a dreamy and creative personality, or anxiety issues may keep a student more in his head than in his body.

Certain mental health issues such as Obsessive Compulsive Disorder, General Anxiety Disorder or Attention Deficit Disorder may also tend to make a student live more in his mind, and less aware of the body.

Trust and Skepticism: If a student continually returns with the same problems in a piece, she may not trust me as a teacher. She may not believe in my suggestions.

Fear: Some students may have played for years with certain impediments such as faulty hand position or posture. To change now means extra work and possible failure. They have achieved some measure of success and are afraid that if they change they will find they have no musical ability. This is of course groundless; any time we give up obstacles, our ability only flowers.

Colorful Personality: A student may be of the opinion that his mistakes and habits show his unique style. That the mistakes are part of a colorful, individualistic musical personality. He might think that removing these traits would make him generic and bland.

This is often true in life. A person might be amused by the fact that he is often late, running wildly like a mad professor, making people wait. Someone else is proud of always interrupting people. He thinks it shows a strong personality and active intelligence; meanwhile people are avoiding him.

Thus, any musical or technical foibles, and personality tics, if they never blossom into some creative statement or spiritual good, are only getting in the way of the true shades of their owners' personality colors.

❧ How to Approach?

It is not always advisable or necessary to tell the student what you perceive as a *spiritual habit.* This can be hurtful and possibly dangerous for your studio, if the parent or adult student decides to leave or take legal action.

But if I am subtle, I can bring up certain trends in behavior without actually discussing them. For example, if a student gives up easily and is generally anxious, I can say, "Your goal is to become tougher, braver, and try new techniques. Don't give up on this new technique just because it is hard."

If I couch goals for their spiritual improvement positively and in the specific context of the music we are playing, the student and parent will accept my comments. If, however, I say you are a fearful person, or your family is out of touch with the physical realm, this would be neither kind, helpful, nor welcome.

Even my simply being aware of these spiritual habits will help the student. I will understand his problems better and be able to come up with appropriate solutions. I can aim all my thoughts, suggestions and musical ideas, in fact my whole being, in the direction of the student's giving up the spiritual obstacle. Then, if I have faith, and the student desires the results that I suggest, there will be a change.

❧ Change Outside of Studio

When a student becomes aware of a spiritual habit and is able to effect change, it often affects her life outside the studio. I have spoken to parents about students and their obstacles. I have found out that the same characteristics were manifested at home. Students who would stubbornly ignore my suggestions also refused to do household chores. Students who are skeptical in lessons are iconoclasts at home. Lack of bravery, easy quitting, propensity to cry, anger issues, procrastination, all are happening outside the studio. Of course that is no surprise.

I like to think that helping the student confront the issue in the studio, alerting the parents to the same issue, and informing them of my discussions with the student, will give the family another perspective on the situation. Then changes, though subtle and slow, will take place outside of the studio.

As long as I am gentle, and have the best musical and spiritual interests for the student in mind, he and his family are usually open to discussion.

Seymour Bernstein, pianist and author of *Monsters and Angels—Surviving the Music Business* and *With Your own Two Hands,* is a great believer in speaking to the person behind the student's mask. I was recently fortunate enough to have a lesson with this great teacher and soul. Before both pieces I made disclaimers. My hands were cold, I told him, I hoped he didn't mind my tempo, and other apologies.

At one point he stopped me and said, "Why are you saying things that detract from yourself? You don't project that kind of person, you are not that kind of person!" At the end of the lesson he praised my music and also my human side. Thus, he did more than make me comfortable playing for him. He also gave me a life lesson. I won't become a more confident person overnight, but his comments, tone of voice and facial expression will stay with me and grow in my memory.

✥ Nobility of the Soul in our Repertoire

Ultimately, as artists, we want to be spiritually strong and upright in order to experience great repertoire. How will I summon the ferocity of Chopin's ballades if I myself am fearful? If I allow myself to be clumsy and overbearing, how will I play his graceful nocturnes? If I am blinkered and stubborn in my dealings with people, how can I be open to poetic, contemplative discussions in his mazurkas? Etc.

All musical problems, including technical and physical, will dissolve if I emulate the noble human qualities contained in these and other great compositions.

GROUP BELIEFS

❧ The Influence of Group Beliefs

Any habit or pattern of behavior is made easier or more difficult by my group beliefs. These are the patterns and preconceptions held by people in my cultural, familial, and social networks.

Following are examples of group beliefs:

On a cultural level, Americans place a high value on independence, even if it means isolation. Other cultures, such as India and some European nations, place a higher value on local community, even if it means sacrificing some freedom of personal choice.

The door is always open in Indian and European cultures. Guests, especially older friends and family, are to be honored and are usually entertained whenever they show up, often unannounced. In America, if you show up without calling, you might be met with drawn curtains.

On a subcultural level, the Lower East Side of Manhattan places a value on the avant garde. In this, the twenty-first century, black clothes, body piercing and tough physical gestures are "in vogue."

Now take the subway to the Upper West Side. Here the wardrobe and accessories from the Lower East Side would be snickered at. A tattooed "dude" with a nose ring, leather shorts and army boots who somehow wandered onto Central Park West would get looks that would say, "Why don't you grow up and wear tweed!"

On a personal level, if someone has friends and family who drink excessive amounts of alcohol, it is easy to join in. And difficult later to abstain.

It is difficult to live in one of these cultures and act in the way of the others.

❧ Reasons for the Influence

There are at least two sources for the power of group beliefs.

One is simply that I might have never experienced other models of behavior and thought. If I have only interacted with our family, or people in my own culture or subculture, and have friends with similar beliefs and patterns to myself, I will not be exposed to new ideas and ways of being.

Secondly, even if I do discover other modes of thought and action, my group will exert a strong influence on my actions and perhaps prevent me from exploring these other ways of being.

The group might sincerely believe it is right and do everything possible to persuade me. Or it might simply be holding onto these beliefs and to me, afraid to let go and to reveal its weaknesses.

૬ Finding or Building My Own Healthiest Group

It is important for my sanity and spiritual health to find immediate social networks that support my healthiest beliefs and practices. If my overall culture does not fill my social or psychological needs, I must find the proper subculture or set of friends. If my friends or family members hold unhealthy beliefs and try to impose them on me, directly or indirectly, it is important to be aware of that and be immune.

Sometimes when I meet old friends, I realize the only thing I had in common with them was our old set of unhealthy group beliefs.

૬ Personal beliefs

Either by changing groups, building new ones, or thinking independently, I must somehow hold the beliefs in my own mind and heart that allow me maximum spiritual and musical growth. I can then be closer to my students and my music, and by example, encourage them to grow in the same way.

THE CATERPILLAR'S FOURTH SKIN:
REMOVING THE BODY
FROM THE MUSIC

After the caterpillar sheds its skin for the last time ... it has no eyes, antennae, mouth, wings, or legs.

> ➤ Life Cycle of a Butterfly, Bellevue State Park Website
> http://www.state.ia.us/parks/lifecycl.htm

When a caterpillar is fully grown it takes time to wander in search of a suitable pupation site.

> ➤ Captain's European Butterfly Guide
> http://www.butterfly-guide.co.uk/life/

Technique, simply defined, is how I move at the piano.

My body will move in the manner required by the music, only if I am listening to my soul and to the soul of the music, and if I am able to eliminate spiritual habits that affect graceful motion.

Often there is blockage in the physical motion at the keyboard. Then there must be an urgency on the part of player, an awareness of proper spirit in his life.

Add to that proper training, and any student — I repeat any student — can acquire advanced, fluid and effective technique.

TECHNIQUE, THE INVISIBLE HAND

Technique, in the proper spirit, is the *invisible hand*, the unseen force. It should be effortless and should leave no signs, only art.

❧ Technique Alone is Amoral

Technical mastery represents my logistical relationship with the music. It makes possible any musical event contained in the score and any idea I have about the score. In this way technical mastery is only a tool, not an end in itself.

A tool is not inherently good in itself. Knowledge and ability, for example, can be used to do harm, and power can be corrupted. The pursuit of these tools is amoral and must be accompanied with good spiritual intention.

In music, an effective technique alone lacks beauty. It must be combined with an equal level of thinking and spirit to have musical value.

❧ Invisible

Therefore technique is invisible and non-existent in the realm of heart and spirit. In the same way, it should be invisible in the physical realm. That is, it should not be noticed. Only the music should be noticed. Clean, solid, and even-toned arpeggios, for example, are not something I "see." I only "see" the music that is in an arpeggiated passage.

I only "see" technique when it is obtrusive, when it is unclean, unclear, uneven or hinders me in any way. Then it becomes an obstacle, a helpless, unwitting agent of destruction or neglect.

Thus technique, overall, has no music in it, spiritually or physically. It is an empty quality, a negative space, in that when it is done properly, it excuses itself, moves out of view and allows the music to flow forth.

❧ Solving Technical Problems

To solve technical problems that arise in the score, I can perceive my technique as words. (This is only an analogy; I am not saying technique has a verbal connection. That is more *phrasing*.) To write clearly, words I choose should be graceful, not too strong or flamboyant, not evident or overshadowing of the ideas. Also, my words and wording should not be weak or faulty.

In the same way that clean, precise and unobtrusive prose serves the intellectual idea, technique must be skillful, subtle and serve the musical idea. Invisible.

The idea of technical invisibility can be applied to all musical circumstances and all technical questions, from the two-note slur to octave scales, to a complicated melodic figure. So, the proper technical solution is that which uses minimum effort, maximum grace, and allows the full throat of the song to be heard.

HOW I FINALLY LET GO OF MY BODY

Technique, as Vladimir Horowitz puts it, is the means. It is the vehicle with which one can be transported to divine places. It is also probably the most common obstacle to musical satisfaction and progress. So many people quit lessons or become frustrated because their technique is faulty. But just about everybody can acquire fluid motion at the keyboard and can play at an advanced level.

I know, because if I can do it, just about anybody can.

I started lessons because my pediatrician told my parents I had bad small motor control. My penmanship was practically illegible and I was awkward and clumsy. Piano lessons did help, but I never really learned solid technique in early years, I am not sure why. It is easy to point fingers, but I will certainly take blame, if there is any to be given. I didn't really practice that much until I was eleven, and when I finally caught fire and started to take piano more seriously, my habits and flaws were already ingrained.

My family had always listened to the serious classics, and dinnertime was accompanied by Brendel, Kraus, Gilels, Serkin, de Larrocha, Rubinstein, Horowitz, and other greats. By the time I got serious about piano, I wanted to play the wonderful pieces they played, but of course my technique got in the way. Although I worked hard and had some success performing (Beethoven's Third Piano Concerto with my high school orchestra, Beethoven opus 53 and Chopin's b-minor Scherzo in my high school senior recital), I was never able to produce a smooth legato or control my sound the way I wanted. In addition, learning pieces took longer than it should have.

In college music school, I encountered more problems, and even stopped repertoire for two years to revamp my technique, as much an ordeal or more for my patient teacher than for myself.

Lesson after lesson my teacher would show me in different ways how I should approach the piano more softly and less woodenly. I played chords slowly, playing from the shoulders. I played intermediate pieces like Schubert impromptus to really concentrate on sound and fluid motion. I would touch his forearm while he played, he would "play the piano" on my arm. I would listen to his smooth, fluid tone and try to imitate. He would even have me do unconventional things like punch the wall and stop my fist just before impact, to introduce softness.

Hour after hour I would spend in the basement practice rooms, shut off from the world and my youth. Instead of developing myself emotionally and spiritually, and connecting to the softness of my soul and body through life experiences, I rammed head-on toward "good technique."

Each night I would often be so frustrated I would punch the locker where I kept my books. By the end of the year the metal was dented with knuckle imprints.

As the two-year experiment drew to a close, and it became apparent I wasn't improving, I withdrew from life. I wouldn't answer calls. I enrolled in computer science course as a "back-up" and spent 24- and 36-hour periods in the computer room working on programs. My best friend and roommate left school and I felt very alone.

I still practiced, but not very effectively. At the jury I fumbled an easy piece.

I don't know why our experiment didn't succeed. He was a concert pianist and great pedagogue, and I really looked up to him and had great affection for him. I was certainly on fire to learn. For whatever reason, I still had uneven legato and a harsh wooden approach, albeit a little less so.

I felt a bit betrayed by the piano. During the stormy years of adolescence and young adulthood, I had always thought the piano would at least give back what I invested in it, even if human friendships sometimes didn't seem to. But now it appeared that wasn't true.

I was wrong, but didn't know it. The piano does give back what you give, and I had been giving the wrong things. I had been straining and forcing, in order to achieve fluidity. Of course this is a contradiction. I had been concentrating on technique, the sound, my body, but not the music. That's backward thinking.

And most importantly, I was not changing as a person. I was still emotionally immature, reserved, self-conscious, stiff and graceless.

❧ Rehabilitation

Help came from surprising places. After music school, disappointed and frustrated, I gave up serious piano pursuits. For musical satisfaction, I strummed a guitar I bought on my street in Queens and wrote songs. After returning to piano a couple of years later, I continued with the "pop" side, singing every day for almost ten years. Although I am not a serious threat to any working singer, I believe this opened my ear up to natural breathing and phrasing at the piano. Through my songwriting, I developed relative pitch and a much greater sensitivity toward sound in general.

I believe this aural sensitivity actually opened my body up. Because the voice is easier to manipulate than piano sonority, I was able to experiment with my singing, sculpting the sound to fit musical intention. And the more control I developed over musical intention, the more my arms and hands reacted on the guitar, to complement the mood of the song. Thus, my singing helped my hands and body become softer, more pliant.

Also, the guitar/song culture is a relaxing, liberating environment. Arms draped over sensuously shaped wood, usually sipping some "recreational" beverage, sitting on a floor or rooftop or in a circle of friends. How different from my solitary days in the practice rooms. And how ironic that in these rooms I was so determinedly trying to gain this freeness of body and musical spirit that finally came with no effort.

I finally learned an important lesson, letting go in order to gain. I am reminded of my friend's two children, each of whom had a dog. The boy would hold the puppy in his lap and cover it with clumsy kisses and hugs. Of course it ran to the sister and her dog every chance it got. The more he tried to force affection on it, the more it resisted. The same is true in music. Straining and forcing your technique to come never works.

♪ A Need to Play

In addition, I believe living on my own in New York, and going into a career transition had a positive effect on attitude toward the piano, in a roundabout way. I was experiencing loss and was encountering grief, although at the time I just felt confused and a bit scared. So, I once more returned to the piano.

I offered to accompany a dance class in return for practicing on the studio's piano. I became friends with the instructor and his wife and after class I would pour my heart out to them on their beautiful Steinway grand. My technique did not exactly improve from an objective standpoint, but I became much more connected to music and to the piano. I think it was because in all my life, playing the piano had been a love labor, an assignment, or a letter grade. But I don't think it had ever been something I *desperately needed* to do. Now, confused, embarrassed and bereft, I finally experienced this need.

I believe that my playing became sensitized as a result of this need to express my feelings of loss and confusion as a young adult. Again, as with singing, my body became more responsive as a reaction to my musical needs.

♪ Dance!

The dance instructor, a wonderful man named Milton Feher, gave me tips on how to accentuate rhythm. He would pass by me and stamp his feet to show me how to land on the downbeats.

Milton also let me sit in on his classes, where we learned how to make our bodies grounded and centered.

We would lie on the cool wooden floor and he would talk us on a "trip" through our bodies. His resonant, mellow voice would make each limb and muscle relax until we felt like puddles on the floor. The studio was in mid-Manhattan, a block from Carnegie Hall and across the street from a fire station. Every time a siren went off, Milton would intone, "Use the sound to relax more."

My work in Milton's classes and my long talks with him helped me become more connected to my body, and gave me more spiritual and physical balance. He was no stranger to transformation. After dancing in the Ballet Russe under Balanchine, he had developed a knee condition. Doctors said he would never dance again. Milton developed his own method of relaxation and body discovery and cured himself. And here he was at seventy-five showing me how to move! Also, his lovely wife Marga made fantastic, unique soups, and their laughter and gentle attitude toward life gave me a spiritual bond that I cherished.

§ Down to Business

After a few years of teaching and many years of these musical and spiritual "sabbaticals," I decided I wanted to really confront "hard tacks" issues in my piano technique. I was fortunate enough to meet a concert pianist, master pedagogue and Tai Chi master at the keyboard.

TAI CHI MASTER AT THE KEYBOARD

Her name is Ena Bronstein Barton. Kind, gentle and pedagogically razor sharp, our study together solved many of my pianistic problems and gave me the ammunition to solve technical problems on my own.

We discussed arm movement. Ms. Bronstein had been a pupil of Claudio Arrau, whose instruction included a unified rotation motion. In all contact with the keys, there is a rounded motion that the arm and hand make. It is up and toward the thumb, then around and across, low, toward the pinky. Clockwise in the left, counter-clockwise in the right.

Every note, chord or phrase used this motion. Watching Ms. Bronstein demonstrate reminded me of Tai Chi, ballet, fencing or any graceful physical art. I found out later that she studied Tai Chi.

I learned that if I played a chord, I could drop my arm weight in while rotating, and then rotate out of the chord. This produced a rounded, deeper tone, not surprisingly. The same circular movements were used with two notes, or a whole phrase.

I was elated. I had finally found an integrated philosophy of technique in which I could immerse myself. I had spent my whole life being told to "Relax!", to connect the notes, to make a rounded sound, but never knowing exactly how! Finally, there were answers. Ms. Bronstein made the comment that I was like a plant that just needed some watering. And our study together provided this relief.

♪ Easy Technique

I believe that my difficulties actually lay in not knowing how effortless good technique really is. I am not referring to the discipline and time required to develop advanced technique. Nor am I saying that everybody is able to play like Horowitz. (For that matter, can anybody play like Horowitz?)

When technique is correct, it provides the most natural and easiest way of playing a passage. Then, there is the least resistance between our bodies and our musical ideas, and technique has achieved its purpose.

And fluid technique saves time. Often many hours of practice are devoted to mastering a passage that could take a few minutes with a different hand position or arm motion.

I think what is difficult is convincing the student of this idea, that graceful technique removes the burden of clumsy playing, uncontrolled sound and unachieved musical ideals. And that if we know the way, and learn to "let go," the music will come.

In this way, technique is the "invisible hand."

Spinning the Cocoon:
Finding Peace Inside and
Outside the Studio

The Monarch Pupa

Although the pupa outwardly looks inert and resting, inside it is a bubbling cauldron of activity as the caterpillar is literally liquefied, then reassembled, over about two to three weeks, into a very different creature. It's is still not fully understood how this process occurs. Some species hibernate in this state, although the transforming chemistry is suspended for most of the winter period in this case.

➤ The Amazing life Cycle of a Butterfly
http://www.butterflies.org.uk/lbh_home/cycle/lifecycl.htm

The student has a true voice that calls to us through all the potential chaos of a piano lesson and of life.

We, as pianists, students and teachers, must find our own peace (still mind), as well as peace in the studio (lesson peace), in order to answer that call.

STILL MIND

My mind expresses my relationship to my own soul, and the souls of my students and my music. If it is inhabited with doubts, paralyzed by fear or clouded in any way with negative or extraneous thoughts and emotions, it limits this relationship.

❧ As Musician

As a musician, I need to "listen" to and understand my own spirit and the spirit of my surroundings. Then, when I play a piece of repertoire, I need to bring what I know about myself and my world to the piece.

I have to be sensitive to all aspects of myself and of the world, including the physical, psychological, emotional. Then I have to be sensitive to all aspects of the piece, including the harmonic, sonic, tactile and psychological.

If my mind is not still, I won't hear my spirit, or that of the world or piece.

If my mind and heart are calm, shutting out the psychic noise of my day, and if I can control the lesson and not be affected by the student's or my errant energy, I have achieved still mind.

♦ Pianist's Canvas

I tell my students to create a canvas of silence before they start to play a piece or their practice. Just like a painter needs a blank, white canvas on which to paint, we need a layer of silence before painting with sound colors. I encourage them to wait several seconds before playing and really hear the silence in the room.

This gives them a chance to quiet their minds and also their bodies. I tell them the silence must also be inside of them. They usually look more peaceful when I say this. I tell them there should not be anything between their music and their minds and hearts.

If a student is experiencing personal problems or has an active body and mind, this is an opportunity to leave that behind. I tell them practice can be an oasis, that we have an obligation to the music to stop thinking about ourselves for a while. Then, the first note and every note thereafter can be a celebration of different tonal colors splashed on the clear canvas of the silence they create.

♦ As Teacher

Still mind doesn't mean I am blank. In fact, I can experience the music and the student much more vividly.

I can throw myself into the moment and immediately regain balance. I can discuss discipline with a student and then smile and continue.

In short, with still mind, I am completely alert and balanced, more connected to the souls of my music, my students and myself.

I can then listen to and nurture the student's true voice, his pure musical intention, unencumbered by all the rest.

TRUE VOICE

Underneath all of the "noise" and "interference," it is important for me to try to hear the student's true voice. That is when the student plays one passage with overpowering tenderness, or her eyes widen when hearing a certain piece she wants to play. This is the student's true voice coming through.

Just as the natural repose of the human soul is upright and pure, I believe that within all music students is the desire to create beauty. They may hide this desire, or inadvertently block it with spiritual habits, but it is there.

It is the student's true voice that we must seek to hear. When heard, we address it and help it grow.

PSYCHIC NOISE

❧ Psychic Noise

Teaching can be frustrating, exhilarating, joyful, and everything in between. And the music we play and teach encompasses the tragic, romantic, melancholy, noble, grand, comic, simple, singing, rhapsodic, and infinitely more aspects of the human condition. So, emotion is our currency, our medium, our tool kit.

It's easy to get caught in this whirlwind of feeling. Like actors, we have to open ourselves to them in order to perform. And like directors, we have to try to coax and win these performances out of our students.

Emotional and personal issues from our personal life can seep into the lesson, destroying lesson peace and our ability to teach with still mind. In the chapter "Find and Maintain Your Peace" I discuss specific ways of eliminating these from our lives.

In this chapter I will discuss some examples of psychic noise and offer some different ways of understanding and deflecting them.

More importantly, I hope to show how we can break down negative emotions into their harmless components.

§ Fear

On an everyday level, we musicians need bravery to continue as practicing craftsmen. At times I have stopped studying or practicing for months or even years. I have often been puzzled by my reaction. Isn't it more logical to try harder when challenged?

It's not that I would find I am less talented than someone else, I already know who I am. Not so much that I would be found out to be a fraud and everybody would sign a petition to stop me teaching piano. I already know I can teach well.

I had been afraid of developing my piano skills and imagination because of what I might find on the journey. It is the discovery process, the self-awareness that scared me. What would each of these steps of the journey say about me? I was afraid to find out, and more, I was afraid of the fear I would feel each time. Afraid of the fear.

§ Useless Baggage

Once I separate fear from my musical pursuits, fear can be seen as simply a character flaw, or a neurosis, or an issue, or whatever label you want to use. Not a musical problem. Therefore, fear has no place in the studio.

Here are some sentences to remember:

We need bravery to admit we don't know something, in order to learn.

We need bravery to admit we need improvement, in order to improve.

There is nothing to fear in our musical pursuits except wasting time.

Fear is simply: *Allowing everyday events and social norms to dictate our thoughts and behavior.*

Overcoming fear is as easy as: *Continuing with a productive life despite everyday events and social norms.*

We might not be able to eliminate fear, because it is so instinctive. But we can refuse to let it control our actions. And, if it is fear based on false expectations, we can expose it as false.

♪ Anger

In our studio, as in life, anger can be healthy. It is a warning signal, that something has been violated. If a student is not reaching his great potential, we have a right as mentors to be angry. If a student has shown disrespect, we have a right to be angry.

But it is not healthy or professional to express this anger in the studio. We are there to guide the students, not express ourselves to them. They are not in a social relationship with us, no matter how close they are.

Therefore anger must be kept to ourselves professionally. We address the cause of the anger and try to eliminate it. We try to lead students to realize their potential or we calmly discipline their behavior.

From a practical perspective, it is unwise to show anger. Then the student knows he has brought us to his level. We lose our standing as an authority.

❧ Outside the Studio

If we feed anger, it will certainly grow and become too strong to control. If we ignore anger, however, it can turn inward. Then we can become depressed. Therefore the best path is to acknowledge it but not harbor it. Deflection is not the same as denial.

Do we deal with the sources of our anger? Absolutely, but in a productive way. If discussion is impossible, accept that, as difficult as it may be.

❧ What is Important

We are musicians and teachers. This is a time-consuming and labor-intensive profession. We do not have time for anger.

Anger is simply: *a human reaction to what we perceive as a wrongful action.*

Anger can be turned to our advantage and then controlled by:

First, acknowledging that there was a violation (thus taking advantage of it as a warning signal);

Second, admitting to ourselves we feel angry;

Third, leaving behind the anger and;

Fourth, correcting the violation.

Learning to not harbor anger is kind of like practicing a Chopin etude in the emotional health world; it can be terrifically difficult. But it becomes easier with practice.

❧ Jealousy

Among performing artists, jealously is an occupational hazard. But it is one of those false emotions, like frustration. It exists only because we let it. Just as frustration in a lesson (discussed later) is expecting where you are to be somewhere else, jealousy is simply: *Expecting who you are to be someone else.*

Eliminating jealousy is as easy as: *Allowing who you are to not be someone else.*

I can't think with someone else's thoughts or play with her style. Nor do I want to.

❧ Doubts, Worries and their Conqueror: Confidence

Frustration and jealousy are *false* emotions; they are caused by false expectations. Either we wish we were somewhere else (frustration) or someone else (jealousy).

Doubts and worries are also false, but in a slightly different way. They are like Chicken Little, running around screaming that the sky is falling. Or like a neurotic, amnesiac big brother who keeps reminding you to get your car fixed long after you've fixed it.

ﾟ Emotions of Inaction

It is sign of their unrealness as emotions that they show up mostly at night, when we have the least contact with our world of action. For doubts and worries are not action oriented, they prey on inaction and cause inaction. If we plan responsibly for what we need to do and carry through on those plans, we don't have the time nor need to have worries or doubts. And, conversely, if we spend our time worrying and having doubts, we won't be able to get on with life.

ﾟ Doubts and Worries

Doubts and worries are created in our minds, but if entertained, they take on a life of their own. They are like unwanted guests at a party, wandering around your living space and criticizing random things. "The carpet is the wrong color," "this chair is too big," "your house is too small," etc. They are useless complaints that don't help us. If you have decided on a course of action based on your true motivations, sound advice, and if necessary, research, proceed and don't second-guess. Only time will inform us of success.

Worries are simply: *Infinitely repeating thoughts on a subject that needs only one set of thoughts and actions.*

Worries can be eliminated as easily as: *Remembering that you already thought through a plan and have put it into action.*

❧ Confidence

At the root of many of these unproductive thought patterns is lack of confidence. Confidence is a coat that we weave out of good, solid materials. The pattern is one of our own invention. The threads, fabric and lining are woven with our work, training, thought, experience and ultimately results. When finished, this coat protects us. (Perhaps coat of armor is more appropriate!)

Mentors and master teachers in our particular specialty can confirm that we are on the right track. Competitions and adjudications can also provide feedback. The student's excitement, motivation and performance quality, together with our own musical progress and the spirit with which we teach also reflect our success.

Confidence is simply: *The confirmed knowledge that you have the ability and motivation to carry out your plans.*

Confidence can be affirmed as easily as: *Seeing that your initial goals are matched by the results of your efforts.*

♭ Keeping Life in Perspective

It's important to remember that our lives are finite. A friend of mine said that he keeps his mortality in mind and that is how he keeps his room clean. Remember the overall context of our lives. Then it is easy to shed useless and unproductive thought patterns in favor of real work and thought. One of the most helpful statements I have ever heard regarding peace of mind was given to me by Seymour Bernstein. I was about to play a Mozart sonata and must have looked distracted.

"What are you thinking right now?" he asked me.

I decided to confide in him. "Well, I made a dinner reservation at the wrong restaurant, and I hope my wife, her friend, and the friend's family like it. I'm also thinking about the car and will it get a ticket? And then..."

He stopped me, held up a finger, looked me right in the eye and said, "Always remember this. This music is more important than you are. This music is more *important* than you are."

Suddenly all my petty personal thoughts vanished.

Instead, there was a clear image of Mozart's timeless music, waiting to be brought to life once more. My playing ceased to be a nervous lesson with a famous master and became one small piece of a worldwide mission.

FIND AND MAINTAIN STILL MIND

Although we know intellectually that many of these negative emotions are useless they are quite often difficult to confront and conquer.

The first step to fighting psychic noise is acknowledgement of its various sources.

❧ Acknowledgement

Acknowledgement is one of the greatest healing forces. Often we hold onto negative feelings and memories because we don't want to admit that they are true. As performing artists, we are prone to perfectionism, which produces wonderful playing and teaching, but when applied to our emotions, can cause us to stagnate. We feel we must be perfect beings and deny our right to be human. Then, because the problem is still there, we invent other reasons for it and it doesn't go away.

For example, one can feel anger at someone for losing touch. One might then invent many reasons why one is angry, instead of saying, "You know, I'm human, and I'm simply upset that you don't spend as much time with me anymore!" You don't need to say it to that person, but by admitting you are human and can be hurt, you can stop thinking about it.

Similarly, depression can be a red flag to us that something is wrong. Sometimes depression is a result of not acknowledging a problem or problems in our lives.

If we identify the source of the problems, even if we cannot immediately address it, we can then at least start to move out of the depression stage.

❧ Different Paths to Peace

After we have acknowledged the sources of our peace blockers, it is then possible to seek help. Help can come from within, but often it must come from an external agent. Psychiatrists, psychologists, social workers, priests, rabbis, ministers, and Zen practitioners can all be those agents.

❧ Therapy or Counseling

Psychological counseling, or therapy, can be an effective way to manage overwhelming and paralyzing emotions. It still holds a stigma in many cultures, and thus many people are discouraged from seeking it. But it is important to remember that therapy and counseling come in many different packages.

In my opinion, everybody could benefit from therapy. I perceive therapists as our advisors, just as heads of state or CEOs have advisors. Isn't life as important to us and our family and students as a company is to a CEO?

Here are some myths about therapy and some attempts to shatter them:

Myth 1 — *Therapy is for weak people.* Not true. It takes a strong person to admit he needs help. And it takes tremendous courage to change negative patterns, either behavioral, emotional or mental. This change is the purpose of most therapy.

Myth 2 — *Therapy is a way of blaming everything on others.* Not true. By getting healthy through therapy, you are actually taking responsibility, seeking to bring positivity into your life, relationships and work.

Myth 3 — *I can straighten out my problems by talking to my friends.* Not always true. Although this is often the case, and it is always good to have a friend you can talk to, therapy is different from the average heart-to-heart with friends. This is called enabling and will cheer you up in the short term, but not help break any patterns. A therapist can get to the roots of why you feel or act this way and help you avoid it next time.

Myth 4 — *I must be really messed up if I'm in therapy.* First of all, not true. There are all kinds of people who are in therapy, from well in normal range to well outside.

Second of all, so what if you are messed up? All our goals are the same: to become healthy.

Myth 5 — *I can't afford it.* But you can. There are all kinds of therapists, from psychiatrists to psychologists to social workers, all with their own rates. Some work for subsidized agencies and offer sliding scale and heavy discounts. And your insurance might cover some of it, although the insurance industry has to wake up and realize that the brain is part of the body.

Myth 6 — *I could never trust a stranger to open up my secrets and concerns to.* But in a way, isn't that what we are asking our students to do, only musically? Of course, you might not be comfortable at first. But trust can be built up and earned, and is, by definition, a risk. Ask a prospective therapist about his confidentiality policies, and if he is professional, he will be glad to reassure you.

❧ Spiritual Help

Maybe you prefer to confide in your priest, minister, rabbi, or other religious leader. Perhaps a Zen Buddhist meditation center or some other form of spiritual activity is your style.

I have not tried meditation much, although I have benefited from reading about it. In *Through an Eastern Window,* Jack Huber talks about meditation. He allows thoughts to float into his mind and not try to block them or notice them. Focusing only on his breathing, he eventually achieves a clear mind.

This has been helpful for me. I have an active mind and many things are always popping into it. By adopting this technique, I am able to "slow things down."

❧ Invent Your Own Mental Health Techniques

When I was a child I had bouts of mild OCD, Obsessive Compulsive Disorder. I never told anyone, of course. I thought I was the only one who had this disorder. I often found myself compelled to repeat actions over and over again.

I would tap out specific groups of numbers, repeat certain words in my head, or visualize different images over and over again. It has affected my test-taking ability and my focus at the keyboard. Growing up I would sometimes spend half the test period working out complex rituals before diving desperately into the exam, trying to catch up. It also put me in embarrassing situations when my classmates saw me doing repeated motions.

Much later, as an adult, I read *The Boy Who Couldn't Stop Washing*, by Judith L. Rapoport. Then I realized I was one of millions, some with much more time-consuming symptoms. My disorder had to do partly with being a nervous personality, and these rituals were simply ways my subconscious allowed me to contain, or to use the clinical word, "bind," this anxiety.

Part of OCD is having intrusive thoughts. Images, words and sounds would come breaking into my rational brain in a very irrational manner. I attribute these to a creative thought pattern, anxiety and to the old rule: "It's just the way it is."

I have invented different ways of dealing with these intrusive thoughts. One came from the idea that *I am what I think.* If I am what my mind is, then to reverse that rule, I can imagine becoming something else, a rock for example, and my mind might become like what a rock's mind would be, if it had one. So I start to imagine I am this grey boulder and my extraneous thoughts become very slow, blank and strong. I can focus on the matter at hand, playing, teaching or sleeping.

This is kind of the flipside to Zen meditation, and I suppose from a meditator's standpoint, it is cheating. But it works for me.

❧ Focus on Specific Tasks

Often, still mind is simply a matter of willing it to happen. One way is to focus on the task at hand.

Grace Ting, M.D., an emergency-room specialist and Raghu Murthy, M.D., now a retina specialist, worked in the same emergency room at Los Angeles County General Hospital. This was no ordinary emergency room.

The second largest hospital in the world, Los Angeles County had frequent gang-related incidents.

Grace gave great advice on how to maintain still mind.

> I was trained to work in hectic environments; the key to remaining calm during a crisis is to focus on simple guidelines. In emergency medicine, for example, the golden rule to stabilization is: ABC (airway first, then breathing, then circulation). This sequential guideline was drilled into me during training; it helps me organize and focus my efforts in every situation, from gunshot victims to stroke patients.

Raghu added some great advice on how to maintain freshness in an often chaotic work environment.

> When you are in this hectic environment, remember you are privileged to be there, that your life, interestingly, is a challenge (not boring), that you can make a difference in someone's life, and that your life has a purpose, specifically- i.e., I need to get this patient to the Operating Room to close his eye, and do all that is necessary to accomplish that purpose.

♦ Yourself and Your Higher Power

Whomever you seek for spiritual or psychological guidance, remember that we can always disagree with them. And we can respectfully leave their counsel and go to another guide. Remember that credentials and reputations mean nothing if their advice is not helping you.

We all have our own true voice that tells us when we are spiritually balanced and when we are not. We don't always hear it, but it is there. Musicians especially have an ear for this voice. After all, this is the same voice that tells us that an interpretation is sincere, true, from the heart and lovely. This voice can help us find a guide who is right for us, and understands what we need. And ultimately, we can listen to this voice for our own guidance.

If all else fails or if I need extra help, I turn to prayer. I know this sounds religious, but please understand that I mean go to your higher power, whoever that is. For myself it is the Holy Trinity. For others it might be Allah or Mother Earth or a Mozart sonata; nobody is to judge.

I pray that I may understand a problem, and find a solution. More importantly, I pray that I may have the right questions to begin with! And my most powerful prayer for *still mind* is to have peace even when there are no solutions or understanding coming. This is the hardest peace to maintain, but sometimes it is the only peace available. Peace in spite of all evidence to the contrary!

Lesson Peace

Once we have achieved still mind in our own lives, it is important to have peace in the studio, or lesson peace.

The first step toward lesson peace is finding the balance point — teaching the student where she is.

✎ Balance Point

If I find that a student does not understand me, or is not able to implement my suggestion, I keep backing up until I've reached the student's balance point. That's the point where a student has the requisite knowledge and skills to comprehend what I am saying, and the confidence to take that small leap beyond.

Balance point is where all productive teaching starts. Then I build from there. Experience will tell me how much of a leap we can make before she is off balance.

Every student, no matter how challenged in different areas, has a balance point. It is up to me as the guide to find it and teach from this point.

If the balance point is not found or is continually ignored, this will erode the lesson peace. Lessons will then become unproductive and negative experiences for everybody. This is when students decide to stop taking lessons, teachers decide they want the student to leave the studio, or bad habits start forming. Lack of motivation, sloppy playing, flawed technique and inattentive practicing result.

I will always achieve lesson peace whenever I realize that real musical learning can happen at any level, with anyone.

♪ Frustration in the Lesson

Certainly one of the biggest threats to lesson peace is frustration. Often I hear from people that they are not patient and could not teach. What they are saying is they don't understand the dynamics of frustration.

The worst part of frustration is that it blocks communication. You no longer hear the student's true voice, the one that calls out even when they are silent, that says, I'm trying, I like this piece, help me play it! Instead you see someone not proceeding in the way you want her to. And if you have displayed even the slightest sign of frustration, the student will interpret it as punishment.

When I get frustrated, I remind myself that I have probably lost the balance point. Again, I keep backing up until I reach it.

Frustration is simply: *Expecting where we are to be somewhere else.*

Overcoming and eliminating frustration is as easy as: *Letting go of the "somewhere else" and addressing where we are.*

There is no repertoire, etude, scale or technique that is so important that it must be learned at the expense of lesson peace. Without lesson peace, there can be no real learning, in a profound and inspirational way. And frustration will always erode peace.

♭ Little Causes for Celebration

We've all had the great lesson. The times when a student shows up and uses a technique I've been trying to sell her for months. Suddenly she is excited because her hands can dance on the keyboard, even in the Czerny. Or, for the first time, she achieves a deep and resonant sonority. Or, she plays the piece with great drama, etc. You feel elated and then...

Now what? The next lesson is not spectacular.

Great moments and little moments. This cycle can be disappointing at times, but only if I let it.

To maintain my excitement as a teacher, to create enthusiasm in the student, I must adjust my perspective. Maybe those moments are not so little. I remind myself that this student is different from the last one. Perhaps she didn't have a breakthrough this week — it can't happen every week. But maybe she was willing to learn a new way to move her arms, or she showed more of an ability to make the right hand sing. Or maybe she simply practiced this week.

All of the above, however small, are causes for celebration.

❦ The Student-Teacher Energy Field

Although not talked about much, I believe there is a phenomenon that could use more research and study, and that is human energy fields. Working with someone at close quarters, at high concentration levels, can bring both our energies crashing into each other. It can be intense. Then multiply that by seven different people in quick succession, and by the end of the night we are often drained.

What does the shared energy field consist of? I have not been able to find a scientific definition, but I believe there are several factors that contribute to it. Personal rhythms, body size, spiritual habits, levels of focus, brain waves, and personalities are all involved. There is also chemistry between us, both of our moods and levels of rest. Then there are random factors such as weather, amount of sunlight and what happens during the lesson.

❦ Lighten the Energy Field

With every instruction I give, there is almost a palpable feeling of connection to the students' reaction. There are times when I am teaching that I feel our minds are "inside of each other." There is a force field that our brains and bodies create, and I start to get smothered. At that point there are steps I can take to literally "clear the air."

I can try to change their mood. I can smile, try humor and praise.

I can try to change the pace, tell them to slow down, or to rest while I demonstrate for them.

I can try to explain it in ways that suit their personality.

The fact that I teach piano gives me a lot of power over the energy field. At any moment if the energy field is going too far in any direction, either heavy or frenetic, I can stop and play a piece to counteract it.

❧ Extreme Differences in Personal Energy Fields

Different personal rhythms, brain waves, and personalities will create different shared energy fields. Often it can be quite extreme. There are ways to try to counteract these radical changes in field strength.

If a student has a frenetic personal rhythm, I can slow my speech down, lower my voice and be silent. I can also slow down my physical actions.

If a student is soft-spoken and has a low-energy field or is tired, I can also turn my "volume" down, going slowly and speaking softly, but not pointedly so as with a frenetic student, whom I am trying to calm.

If a student is shy and self-conscious about her playing, I can back my chair away or sit on the far side of the room. Then I can "fold my body in," and literally make myself smaller. Posture and position in the room can have a big effect on shared energy. If a student has a joyful energy, I can turn it up again, and really share humor and enthusiasm with her.

In general, I can use my body position, motions, voice, face, mood, and personal rhythm to affect the field so as to create some compatibility with the student and also make equilibrium in the studio.

♪ The Teacher's Energy Field

Of course, I have my own personal rhythm. I must be careful to present a polished version of myself, no matter what my energy actually is. I must not dress randomly. I must be poised and in control of my movements. Then, the student can focus on the music.

It is also important to show them how to approach the piano, with controlled body and thoughtful mind.

Finally, if I maintain a consistent energy field in the studio, I can build trust with the student.

♪ Maintaining an Energy "Shield"

At times I cannot control the shared energy field. Then, I must try to protect myself.

There are some great visualization exercises to clean shared energy fields that are too heavy or negative, that I found at *thedance.com,* a Web site on Wiccan. Wiccan is a nature religion. It is kind of a holistic, spiritual philosophy with costumes.

You can send the energy down through the chair, into the floor, into the earth. You can visualize different colored light surrounding you. Blue light supposedly keeps bad energy out, white light only lets in good energy, and purple light purifies the whole field.

It doesn't matter whether you believe in these specific principles. I find that simply visualizing the energy draining away or a shield of light going up really makes me calm.

❧ Positive Impact

The draining effects of shared personal energy are lessened if we know we are having a positive impact.

Laurie Powsner, a grief therapist, says that she is less affected by negative energy when she is making a positive impact. "Even though the person is dying and it's sad and tragic, that part can't be changed, and I've helped make the best of the bad situation," she explains.

❧ Maintain Lesson Peace

We can maintain lesson peace, if we: find the student's balance point and teach from there, remember that frustration is usually caused by losing the balance point, remember to celebrate little moments, be aware of our shared energy field, and stay focused on specific items and on the results. Then whatever happens in the studio will depend only on our teaching and the student's sincere efforts.

DISCIPLINE FOR THE COMPLETE ARTIST

Children love justice, adults love mercy.

~ Unknown

❧ Justice and Strength

In the Kabbalah, the Jewish symbol for the Unnamable higher power has equal parts of love and justice. Love, compassion and forgiveness acknowledge humanity, but justice gives us strength.

❧ Compassion as Teacher of Truth

I cannot deny students their humanity. If I brutalize them, that would mean denying that they are still alive, denying that their souls are still receiving messages and forming according to their surroundings. If I want to inculcate in my students an artist's soul, they need to be soft and open in order to sympathize and empathize. They need to be compassionate to the fact that other people are alive and experiencing life.

If we traumatize them with excess in our reactions, we are denying the humanity of the student and ourselves. We are saying, my soul is not alive, your soul is not alive, and you are not human right now. This is, of course, a lie.

If we speak or act too harshly for what the situation calls for, we are inappropriate and this is a lie. We are not reacting in exact proportion to the event.

A lie can never be artistic. And bad attempts at art will always be lies. A true interpretation of Chopin's *Ballade in g minor*, for example, will acknowledge the tragic nobility in the opening, the fatigue of the hero starting to tell his "ballad" on returning from his adventure. Then there must be infinite grace at the transition from the angry g minor opening to the peaceful B-flat interlude.

If the player performs these without knowledge of the importance of the journey, blithely and only for technical impressiveness, then he is saying the piece is only about the exhilaration and effort of the journey, not the lessons learned. This is a lie. It is sometimes called a "shallow" or "too technical" performance. A true performance is called "profound." It is true to the experience of the composer, of the character portrayed in the composition, and to the performer.

If we react to the student and to life in such a way that acknowledges the true nature of things, we are teaching truth and art.

✦ Justice as Teacher of Strength

The main difficulty in being an artist is determining how to open ourselves to others and still protect ourselves from being stolen from and violated, spiritually or in any other way. How do we show our willingness to understand, but still maintain confidence in our own artistic choices, especially in the face of undue criticism and ridicule?

The artist must be willing to make ridiculous artistic choices, and also ones that upset conventional thought and sensibility. He must be brave enough to face the reaction to his choices. This includes his own reaction. He may hate his art at times. He must have the vision and bravery to see that the ridiculous and insane-looking art he has just created can be refined. Later, it may still be ridiculous and insane, and often art is.

An artist must be ready to appear arrogant or incorrect in his assumptions.

We as teachers can help build this bravery by showing a strong front in our firmness and discipline.

✦ Combining the Truth of Compassion with Strength of Justice

In the *Art of War*, Sun Tzu and his commentators say: "A surrounded army must always be given a way out. *Show them a way to life so they will not be in the mood to fight to death.*"

If in our criticism, scolding and discipline of students, we show them that there is a way out, that if they behave and practice correctly, they will progress, they will seek this. If discipline is given chaotically and too heavily, the student may despair and not believe there is a positive option. Then he will not grow. And it is likely he will resist you even more; he will *be in the mood to fight to the death.*

If I show active love immediately after a scolding, the student will see that we can share joy with each other no matter what he has done, so long as he changes and acts positively and professionally.

Being compassionate with the student and acknowledging her humanity at all times, even when scolding, will allow her to grow and be positive in her education. Growth is possible only when we acknowledge that her soul is alive, and teach it to be strong.

Soul Food

Therefore those skilled at the unorthodox are infinite as Heaven and Earth, inexhaustible as the great rivers. When they come to an end, they begin again, like the days and months; they die and are reborn, like the four seasons.

~ Sun Tzu

My soul, mind and heart are composed of what happens to me and the insight I gain from these events. For that reason, I seek out experiences that will feed my artistic sense. And if an experience has nothing to do with music, or even if it is negative, I try to find meaning in it, so that I can constantly learn and grow.

♭ Artistic Nourishment

Because songwriting and singing helped me learn about cantabile phrasing and drama, I listen to vocal music a lot, classical and popular. If the radio is tuned to a "bubblegum teeny-bop" station in the car or at a store, then I can learn what some students are listening to.

Even if an experience is not directly related to music, I am benefiting from the feeling or new insight it gives me. Reading is an activity that inspires me artistically, even though music might never be mentioned. Recently I read *Yellow*, a novel by the great Don Lee, winner of the Hemingway/PENN award for fiction. Here he gives a wonderful description of a master woodworker:

> On first sight, the chair's design wasn't that special — blocky right angles, thick Mission-style slats — but its beauty lay in the craftsmanship. Dean used no nails or screw, no dowels or even glue. Everything was put together by joints, forty-four delicate, intricate joints, modeled after a traditional method of Japanese joinery dating to the seventeenth century, called sashimono. Once coupled, the joints were tenaciously, permanently locked. They would never budge, they would never so much as squeak.
>
> What's more, every surface was finished with a hand plane... He could pull a block plane over a board and produce continuous twelve-foot-long shaving, without a single skip or dig, that was less than a tenth of a millimeter thick — so thin you could read a newspaper through it.

The parallels between this artist's woodcraft and classical piano are obvious. But beyond the subject matter, the writing itself is finely crafted, in much the same way the fictional chairs are. Tight, lean prose, with just exactly the right words to convey the story. I can practically feel the smooth wood and see the dovetail joints. Like a gourmet and healthful meal, this paragraph leaves me better as a person. Nourished artistically, filled with the joy of sharing someone's creation, I return to the studio refreshed and exhilarated.

✎ "Those Skilled at the Unorthodox are as Infinite as Heaven and Earth"

At a recent faculty meeting we discussed how to avoid burnout. We decided that engaging in activities outside of music was a good way to replenish ourselves.

I find I learn a lot about teaching piano from subjects and people outside of the field of music. As Sun Tzu says in the above quote, when I think in an unorthodox manner, it expands my perspective to infinity. And my musical ideas are stronger when reaffirmed in outside areas.

✎ Not in a Vacuum

Many students believe that the only door to great repertoire is the one that opens to the practice room. I must guard them against this belief, through word and action.

I encourage students to read poetry, literature, and watch great movies. I tell them that artists such as Picasso and Monet influenced composers because often painters are bolder as personalities, so they anticipate musical trends with their own innovations. I remind them of historical trends — how, for example, the Romantic 19th century was a reaction to the Age of Enlightenment. I talk about Schumann's ambivalent psychological states to add historical context to the colorful personalities he invented.

I bring in analogies from our own lives, so that a piece is not simply about the phrasing, dynamics, fingering, etc. I engage the student in brief discussions of various life topics, mostly brought up as analogy to something in our musical work. In this way, he will build up an awareness of life issues that may arise in repertoire, a vocabulary of life experience and emotional reaction to that experience.

I want the student to see music as part of the world of art, part of history, and as a reflection and distillation of life. When I see meaning in all of my experiences, both musical and other, I can pass this on to students and help them build aesthetic sense, original thinking, and an overall fresh perspective.

In The Chrysalis:
Transformation

Once the caterpillar has transformed into a pupa a remarkable process occurs, transforming the contents of the pupa into an adult butterfly. This can take as little as two weeks, but some species over-winter (hibernate) in this stage, only hatching in the warmth of spring. As the pupa is unable to avoid any potential predators they tend to be quite well camouflaged, indeed some are formed under the ground.

Just before the adult butterfly hatches, the pupal skin becomes transparent and the wing pattern is visible inside.

> ~ *Captain's European Butterfly Guide*
> http://www.butterfly-guide.co.uk/life/

Transformation is always there for us; we can always seek it. And mastery is possible within all of us.

By seeing the musical tools of rhythm, sound production, and phrasing as different aspects of our organic selves and our souls, it is possible to access them on a high level.

Dynamics of Transformation

What is involved in profound change? First, as piano teachers and spiritual guides, we help the student see what is possible. Then we empower him to make it happen.

❧ Create a Vision of Musical "Wellness"

Native American shamans start their healing by helping the patient to see himself or herself as well. They start from a position of faith, from the premise that the patient is inherently well. When the patient begins to believe this also, he can help the healer work toward a cure.

Similarly, I believe that a piano student is inherently musical and capable of becoming a fine pianist. I have an innate faith in her musical wellness. My job is to help her believe in this vision and to try to make it happen.

❧ Giving up Ownership of the Vision

Greg Burnham, a former adult student of mine, is the chief technology officer for the Port Authority of

New York and New Jersey. When Greg was hired for his current position, a newspaper profile noted that he was good at "building a consensus" for change. In this Greg has exceeded expectations, to say the least.

Under his coaxing and guidance, the New York City subway system is working on a smart card payments system to make public transit easier for commuters. Under his watch, the EZ-Pass electronic toll system is being extended to airport parking, making parking at the New York airports a "breeze."

I was lucky enough to teach Greg for a couple of years. As a busy professional, he didn't always practice as much as he wanted. But he was always deeply connected to his pieces and showed signs of a major transformation in sound production.

"It's not really possible to convince someone to change their traditional thinking and go along with an innovative plan. They must convince themselves," Greg told me by e-mail. "The challenge for a leader is to get others to convince themselves. One way to start is to get them to see that an alternative is possible, that the future could be different, that the future could be better, and that they could contribute."

"A consequence of this approach is that the leader must be willing to let others be part of the innovation, to help shape it, and to help make it happen. In other words, the leader must be willing to give up ownership of the innovation. It's a tricky business."

Knowing Greg, I can see why he is so effective at getting people on his side. He has a leader's "look," tall, muscular and elegant. But when he talks, the impression is of gentle, almost boyish enthusiasm. Once, when I mentioned that I had lived in the same Queens neighborhood he grew up in, his face dissolved into a grin and reverie. He then told me a couple of stories about growing up there. His air of authority and intelligence combined with child-like wonder makes him a perfect advocate for change. He is able both to imagine what could lie ahead and also to get past people's personal defenses and cynicism.

❧ Empower the Student to Change

Students are all resistant to change, for many reasons. Some may be independent and stubborn. Others might be fearful of giving up old habits. Some are fearful of success; if they give up old patterns, what excuse will they have for failure? Others might be afraid of the effort involved.

It is important to help the students see themselves as capable of change. To do this, I must, as Greg says, make them equal partners in the process.

The Alternatives to Violence Project workshops were started by the Quakers to help prison inmates change their patterns of violence and anti-social behavior. Violent offenders often have deeply engrained behavior patterns, stemming from, among other things, a lack of community sense and lack of certain skills such as conflict resolution and problem solving. AVP workshops develop a sense of community and give them options for confronting problems.

The people who run the workshops call themselves *facilitators*, and they use games and round-circle discussions to give the participants respect and dignity. When the inmates see that they have a say in what happens there, they come back, sometimes becoming facilitators themselves.

"To make them realize they are worthy of respect is a great gift for them," explained Rudy Cypser, lead facilitator for AVP workshops and co-director of NY-CURE, a prison reform organization. "They realize this is their thing, not our thing."

Dr. Mehl-Madrona shares this philosophy in treating patients. "I play powerless. I reflect back to them. I can't make them do a thing," he said, meaning 'without their help'. Instead, Lewis told me he uses stories, suggestions and other "tricks" to induce patients to begin the work of healing.

He referred to the Native American story about Coyote stealing fire, which was being guarded by Turtle. Coyote is a tricky animal, who can play dead and fool hunters. In Native American mythology, he is both clownish and wise. In this story, he tricks Turtle. Dr. Mehl-Madrona likens this to how he can trick a patient into letting down his defenses, into letting go of old beliefs and patterns. Trick him into getting well.

♪ Teacher as Catalyst, Not Answer

As a piano teacher, I can never solve a student's problem and make him improve without his help. But I act as a catalyst for change, if I have a strong faith that change is possible and if I can convince the student to share in this faith and take positive action.

Waiting

My music is always waiting for me. Like spiritual awareness, physical fitness, or theoretical knowledge, my music is within me, waiting to be touched upon. Deeper layers of understanding in my playing, higher levels of attainment in technique, greater beauty and strength in my tone, more poetry, more singing, more feeling of epic scope, more nobility, greater sorrow, they are all there waiting to be discovered and implemented in my music.

At different times in my life I have gone back to dig deeper, in various ways, to find musical resources I didn't know I had. These are followed by times when I doubt there is more there to be mined.

It is during these periods of doubt that I mistakenly believe I am waiting for my music, instead of it waiting for me. It is an important distinction. To wait for something implies that it may not come. A more powerful thought is that I can seek it at any time and it can be reached.

RHYTHM AND THE
FUNDAMENTAL PULSE

❧ Temporal Relationships

Rhythm is our temporal relationship with music.

We all have a temporal relationship to life, our own personal rhythm. This is reflected in how we move, speak and act from moment to moment. Some people have a frantic rhythm, others languorous, still others jerky, etc.

The variations in rhythm from person to person are caused by the different layers of interruption between our fundamental pulse and ourselves. The layers include how we think, our emotional make-up, our attitudes, our physicality, our surroundings, everything.

❧ Fundamental Pulse and the Layers of Interruption

The fundamental pulse within everybody is a perfect rhythm, a pulse that resonates with nature. This is obvious when people are stimulated by a particular rhythmic pulse, either music or clapping or speaking.

My job as a piano teacher, then, is to help the student go through these layers of interruption, find his fundamental pulse. In the beginning this might be as simple as the student clapping with a metronome or walking to a steady beat.

What's important is that the student physically and mentally shut out all his layers of interruption and focus on his own resonance with a pulse.

♭ Man-Made Rhythms

Then it just a matter of imposing the man-made constructs of musical note values on our fundamental pulse.

I know that it is possible for all students to achieve this accurately and with natural feel. After all, they speak in complex, man-made rhythms and still have a natural feel. Even physical actions such as opening a combination lock, tying shoes, or starting a car have a series of rhythms that is complex, but that we do the same every time with great accuracy and grace.

♭ New Language of Rhythm

The student must first ignore all layers of interruption and focus on his fundamental pulse. Then, with my help, he can learn the new language of musical note values and use it to express this pulse.

Sound, Our Sensorial Connection to Music

My sound represents my *total sensorial relationship* with my music.

- I feel the subtle interplay between relaxation and tension in my body while touching the keyboard.
- I see the "colors" the sound produces, and various images.
- If a player has a taste-and-smell reaction, this can come out in the sound.
- Of course the final guide is the ear.

The ideas and feelings I want to express will direct the sound. But producing the sound is a physical, sensing activity, even if sight, smell and taste, in the context of piano, exist partially in the imagination.

♭ Touch

It is difficult to explain how the piano can change sound. It looks immutable, unchanging, machine-like. The keys go down and a note comes out the back, like a musical vending machine. But if a student remembers that she is half the instrument, the *humano* part of the *pianohumano*, she can conceive of a piano's sound being controlled.

Also, producing lovely tone simply by ear is, in the beginning, very hard. A student will not have the touch memory bank of what movements of the arm, body and hand will produce which sonority. She has not yet created her palette of tone "colors." So beginning tone production is better approached internally, from the point of view of how it feels in the body.

When I hear students who have beautiful tone, I know that their teachers addressed this subject. When I hear harsh or indifferent tone, the teacher either did not discuss it or was not able to reach the student. Every student is capable of producing lovely tone.

The idea that the piano's tone can be changed is really a radical idea from the point of view of a six-year-old. But it must be introduced early on, so that students can attune their bodies to their own sounds.

I never developed a consistently pleasant tone in my early years. The subject was talked about and I listened to Rubinstein, Horowitz and other masters and savored their rich sounds. But somehow I was never able to connect my body to my sound.

Much later, with the help of Ms. Bronstein, I finally learned how my arms and hands should feel when producing a deeper, more resonant sound. Ms. Bronstein advocates the use of the arm's weight, controlled by the upper arm and torso, a philosophy espoused by her teacher, Claudio Arrau. We worked on the "controlled drop." I would drop my arm into the key, relaxed and weightless, but at the same time control it for intensity, speed and the rounding motion at the bottom. As analogy, I dropped my arm into her hand and was instructed to "give my weight like putting a baby down," to completely and gently release my arm's weight. At first it was difficult.

The movement of the arm is a rotation, so that the arm and wrist are rotating into the bottom of the key and coming out in a rounded motion. I was told to imagine jumping into a pool and having the water let me sink in for a bit, then buoy me up again, in a fluid, rounded manner. I was to transfer this fluidity to all motions on the keyboard.

Another visualization was to aim my energy, like rays of light from my fingertips, through the keys and reaching the floor and below.

For the first time I had a specific plan of action for sound production. Of my three hours a day of practice, I spent almost an hour happily dropping my arms into various single notes and chords around the keyboard. This landscape, the piano keyboard, had always been foreign to me. Now I had a roadmap and went exploring.

Ms. Bronstein told me to read a book, *Zen in the Art of Archery*, by Eugen Herrigel. She had read it as a pupil of Maestro Arrau. The author was a philosophy professor who went to Japan to study Zen with a master archer. He thought he would do some interviews and be back in Germany after some months. Instead, the master handed him a bow, and five years later the author had become a master archer himself.

One of the Zen principles discussed in the book that really helped me understand tone production was the idea of the "It" spirit. The archery students spent the first several months learning only to release the string, with no arrow. The proper release was one that the student did not entirely perform himself. He would release little by little until at the last moment, the "It" spirit would move through the student and release the string. The student was not responsible for the success of the "shot" and was instructed to not rejoice, only to thank "It."

It was a paradox that I appreciated, while relaxing my arm and letting it drop, but still controlling it. Performing the motion hundreds and thousands of times, I was able to better reconcile my physical control with my "letting go."

Another story in the book struck me. The professor challenged his master and said that perhaps it was just practice, and not any spirit "It" that enabled the teacher to hit the bull's eye. As a response, the master met his pupil at night in the shooting range. Placing only a candle near the target, he shot a bull's eye. Then, blindfolding himself, he shot again and this time split the first arrow.

This convinced the philosopher and impressed me with the startling idea that sound production was something I could control from inside my body. Any physical mastery that led to good tone could be felt internally, controlled by *memorized physical responses to the sound*.

My discovery was electric. Of course I had to tell everybody about the book and reread parts of it many times, always connecting passages to new discoveries I made in my roaming "tone explorations" during warm-ups.

My tone became warmer and more rounded. I was astounded, gratified, and finally just relieved to find that my tone was pleasant and at times even lovely! Although it did not stand out yet as a feature of my playing, at least it did not get in the way of my expression of musical ideas. This was a start, one long awaited.

❧ How it Feels is How it Sounds

I try to help students build a memory bank of how their hands and arms feel and to memorize the correlating sounds that these physical feelings produce. I tell them that how they feel is directly related to how they sound.

To build this bank, I teach students to manage their body motions. To release excess tension after playing a note and in between notes. Any tension that they retain should be purposeful. I have them make a fist and relax and memorize how this relaxed forearm feels. To touch my arm when playing a chord and feel how the tension is naturally released. To feel soft fingers when they want soft sound, steely fingers when more projected tone is needed, etc.

Alexei Bukreev, Professor of the Ural State Conservatory in Yekaterinburg, says that once a student discovers he can experiment with sound, he will enter this universe and never leave it.

I try to introduce this universe to a student as early as I can, with as many different physical reference points as he is able to perform. Then we can work on refining his "colors" based on musical ideas.

♦ The Secondary Sound Senses

Sound production is primarily affected by the senses of touch and hearing. These are the primary sound senses.

On a secondary level, sound also involves sight, taste and smell. These senses are not literally "ignited" in the way they are when we see light, or taste and smell food. They are sparked on a psychosomatic level, in some part of the mind. But in its own way, that is very real and physical, not merely analogy.

I see keys in different colors. A major is a bright red, A-flat a deep, rich red. D major is a pale yellow, D-flat a darker yellow. G major is light green, G-flat major is darker green. B major is bright orange, B-flat is dark orange. C major is white, E-flat is black, F has a bluish tint.

So, certain chords will retain the color of their corresponding key; A-flat chords are red, for example. The opening and ending of Chopin's *"Harp" Etude*, in A-flat major, is awash in brilliant billowing swirls of deep red, and of course other colors.

These colors are not analogies or word pictures I use to help bring out different sounds. They are real visual images. I saw them when I started the piano at age six, but of course with no sound awareness in my own playing, I was not able to implement them. They were just there.

❧ Acknowledge Colors in Score

Now I am able to use them to make different tone textures based on chords. I help students see differences in harmonies and reflect them in their playing.

I show them how texture, spacing of voices within the texture, thickness of chords, number of voices, and register, all dictate our sound. I tell students that a master composer does not need to ever write in dynamics, and an aware performer does not need them. The music has already revealed dynamics through various combinations of these elements. We shade in different "hues" in order to acknowledge these changes.

♮ Musical Ideas are the Master

A student should develop the awareness and memory of different physical impulses and the sound they produce. Then he should open all his senses as extra "feelers" for sound. In reading a score, he should acknowledge the changes in texture, register and harmony.

Then he can use his sensitive sound to enhance his musical ideas, the ultimate guide for all his experiments in sonority.

PHRASING

Phrasing represents our vocal relationship to the music. The musical phrase in piano music represents everything we do with our vocal equipment to express our thoughts and our emotions.

♫ Equipment

The piano student must have a fluid technique and awareness of sound. These are like good breath control and vocal tone for a singer or speaker.

♫ Verbal Expression

The student must be comfortable talking and expressing himself intellectually, or at least aware of the possibility of verbal self-expression in its many variations. This will help him inflect various parts of the phrase to make an intelligent musical statement.

Often we talk about singers as models for phrasing in piano. But an introspective, contemplative work, for example a Chopin mazurka, a Bach invention or fugue, or works by Bartok, will require more of a sense of speaking than singing. They are trying to figure things out, contemplate, ruminate. The performer must be able to follow these circuitous and discursive lines of thought and "speak" them.

Of course this first requires that he can think things through intellectually, be circuitous, discursive, and eventually articulate a conclusion in words and thoughts.

♪ Emotional Awareness

Pianists are not usually flamboyant or overt with their emotions in life. But the student should at least be able to identify emotions to himself, and must feel an urgency to express them on the piano. This will lead to sensitive phrasing.

This part of phrasing had always eluded me as a piano student. Lacking a fluid technique meant I could not phrase consistently, but I think it was more a lack of emotional awareness. I don't really know why. I had plenty of emotions and was really passionate about piano.

Perhaps it was my general anxiety level that kind of paralyzed or stiffened my ability to emote. I had always been fearful and anxious, and going to music school had been one long experience of stress, doubt and insecurity.

This stress vanished when I graduated. Moving to New York and giving up piano, I proceeded to take on jobs I hated and live in bohemian (read "miserable") quarters. As I recounted in an earlier chapter, I returned to the piano as a pianist in a dance class. For the first time, I really felt an urgent need to express myself through playing.

Finally finding an awareness and connection to my feelings, and discovering an urgency to play, I was able to express myself through sensitive phrasing.

❧ Nature as Model

An important goal for the piano student is to make his piece come alive, to make it part of the natural world. Therefore his own body and other aspects of nature can be models for phrasing.

A piano student should be aware of his own breathing and body rhythm. Then, he can emulate his body's various fluctuations in tempo, pauses and accelerations in the music.

Examples of other parts of nature are gravity (a bouncing ball is a good model for a natural *accelerando*), the gentle, hypnotic motion of waves, and the gradual fading of the sun at dusk.

❧ Voice as Physical Extension of our Emotions

Listening to vocalists is one of the most important parts of a piano student's education.

The human voice is a unique musical instrument. It is an integral part of the human body and human experience. Even without words, our voice reacts to situations with emotion and meaning.

When we touch something hot, we shriek! When we experience annoyance we involuntarily groan. When something doesn't make any sense, we exclaim, "huh?"

Thus, the voice is part of our body's involuntary emotional responses. It is a fundamental way that humans experience and express emotion.

If she dares, a piano student should actually sing with her voice. This is, of course, frightening for most pianists. And many people say they don't have a good voice. Yet that is simply not true. Almost everybody has a tolerable speaking voice, capable of expressing a wide range of feeling.

♭ Student Finds His Voice

When the piano student has good equipment and connection to his verbal and emotional sides, he will be capable of lovely phrasing. Then he can learn to sing the phrase, and experiment to find his own particular taste.

MASTERY

We are all masters of some sort or another. Even the lazy man is a master. He masters a comfortable position in a chair, fixes his mind on a comfortable point and goes about trying to maintain happiness in this manner.

Mastery is never out of reach. As a teacher, I invite my students to achieve mastery in music. Then, we must aim our bodies and minds in that direction, just as the man in the chair aims at pure relaxation.

A student is masterful *right now* if she adopts an attitude of masterly practice, listening and openness to change.

BUTTERFLY EMERGES:
THE ARTIST'S PATH

The usual first evidence of the butterfly being ready to emerge is the translucency of the pupa skin showing the coloring of the wings beneath. When the pupal skin splits, the limp, damp butterfly crawls out — now with compound eyes, a proboscis for feeding and very clearly six legs — the initially stubby wings are expanded by pumping blood into them and using gravity to help them enlarge.

A little warming in the sun and it is ready to fly off to feed and mate.

~ *The Amazing life Cycle of a Butterfly*
http://www.butterflies.org.uk/lbh_home/cycle/lifecycl.htm

When our desire for change, beliefs about ourselves, communication, peace of mind and basic organic skills are in place, we can ascend to the highest level of piano playing, the artistry of interpretation.

To continue to grow in my music, I must maintain faith. Practice is the active, musical expression of this faith.

Music Theory and the Student's Spirit

I try, when teaching harmony, intervals, scale degrees and other theory topics, to show the psychological impact and spiritual meaning of these topics.

Often students are turned off to theory because:

- It is explained like math problems, as dry exercises done with a pencil, minus heart.
- The teacher doesn't like theory either, because it was explained to him that way!
- The teacher really loves theory, but doesn't think the student will understand how exciting it is until later.

Wrong, I say! Theory is exciting from the very beginning. We are teaching students how music works, not as a math problem, not as a magic trick, but as it relates to us and affects us on a fundamental, emotional and dramatic level.

❧ Tonic, Dominant

In teaching beginning harmony I need not ignore how momentous and amazing the tonic and dominant are! They are, after all, the basic plots for all of the history of western music, including classical and popular. Isn't a symphony's whole goal to "get back home," to quote a Beatles song? This sounds simplistic, and it is, but it also isn't.

I always tell students what my high school English teacher told us. There are only two plots: someone comes to town or leaves town. And that is really only one plot, isn't it? Anyway, the same is true in tonal music. Just about every tonal composition starts and finishes on the tonic. And all the meanderings in between are what make composers different. But the intent of all music that students play and listen to is to "go home again."

So I explain tonic as the home. I will play a tonic chord a few times, whether in a random chord progression or in a piece.

Now, the dominant is the force that brings the piece home. It is the love interest, or the money, or the desire for revenge, whatever brings the main character into town, her new home. See, I tell them, can't you hear the tension, the attraction, the pull, the desire between the dominant and the tonic? Of course they can.

So, watch in your pieces for this "plot" to take place. Just as in all movies, there is a conflict, an urgency, then an action, so in all pieces is there a struggle to get somewhere and finally a force that wins the struggle. Well, that somewhere is the tonic and the force is the dominant.

And there's never anything dry about love, revenge, fortune, conflict and eventual triumph, all present in the dominant-tonic relationship.

♸ Complete the Script

Later, I introduce the subdominant as the force that pulls us away from home. Even later, depending on the student, I will show that all chords fit into the three types, tonic (home — including, submediant and mediant) subdominant (away from home — including supertonic) and dominant (tension — including leading tone harmonies, dominant sevenths and others).

♸ Intervals

I always personalize intervals, to get inside their minds and to get the students in there, too. Of course repetition and comparison to songs that use particular intervals are solid learning methods. But if a student is familiar with the emotional connotations of intervals, she will have a head start on phrasing and creating character in her repertoire.

> ❧ Major thirds are sweet, and sound like your
> parents singing harmony, don't they?

- Major sixths are sweet also, and full of hopeful longing, especially ascending.
- Minor sixths are a bit more jaded, cynical, sad, knowing. Ascending, they are questioning in a pathetic way, descending they are a bit pessimistic. They also remind me of classic architecture, like on New York's Riverside Drive. Don't ask me why.
- A major seventh is outrageous! It is like an incomplete thought, almost arcing up to an octave, but forgetting what it had to say at the last second. Played as a chord it is strident and hostile, but played softly it sounds dreamily hip, like a song from the seventies.
- Fifths are square and strong, they can be neutral and block-like.
- Fourths have a military feel to them, like trumpets. Also, they can be celebrational, as in the *Wedding March* by Wagner.
- Major seconds sound close together, clustered, a bit harsh, perhaps also a bit spicy.
- Minor seconds are like a pinch, they are anxious, like in the theme from the movie *Jaws*.
- Augmented fourths are mysterious and open a world of ominous possibilities. This is of course why they are favorites of modern composers; that is the modern world.

↝ Minor thirds, when part of a minor triad, are
dark, compressed, sad, thoughtful, intimate.
When heard as the top of a major interval, they
are airy, breezy, lovely, like an impressionist
painting of a woman hanging laundry by the sea.

❧ Psychoharmonics

I like to introduce harmony through the repertoire
because it is there that chords live and breathe, wear the
elegant spacing given them by the masters, and inhabit a
specific emotional context. Chords written in block
whole notes on white manuscript paper can desiccate
harmony for students. It is kind of like looking at ink
drawings of animals as opposed to taking a safari.

In Chopin's *Prelude in B minor,* the opening phrase
announces the tragically resigned B minor tonic with
an arpeggiated left-hand figure.

Then, the melody strikes a tone of sudden optimism
with the hearty sounding *G major* arpeggio. The student can acknowledge this change by playing the G major harmony with more fullness, maybe more brightly,
maybe a bit louder. If the student recognizes this G major harmony as a change to more hopeful sound, he can
render the phrase more poignantly.

Later, in the middle section, the music toys with
bringing us home to B minor, but repeatedly ends up
sliding into G major at the last second.

Here the pianist somehow registers that surprise (or is it disappointment?) in his playing, by a subtle mixture of pauses, pressing harder, deeper tone, etc. We want to go to the home chord, or tonic, but are interrupted by the surprise chord, the G major.

When this passage finally lets us go to the tonic, there is a palpable sense of relief. The student can engineer a tasteful increase in tension over this passage, based specifically on the knowledge of the push and pull of the various harmonies and their continued failure to bring us home, to resolve to a tonic.

The eventual resolution to tonic also makes a spiritual statement for the student. In the start of the piece, B minor was felt as melancholic, perhaps a repressing harmonic environment, the G major the liberating one, free, full of fresh air and sunshine.

In the passage above, however, G major is seen as the chord blocking us from reaching home. G major was perhaps initially attractive, but only falsely so. B minor, for all its apparent gloom, here becomes our soul's true state.

Studying the vagaries of the harmony can thus help a student learn the underlying musical psychology and spirituality of his repertoire, enhancing his playing, appreciation of the piece and, most importantly, his understanding of life.

INTERPRETATION AS
STUDENT-HERO'S JOURNEY

Interpretation represents the relationship between the student's self and the character of his music.

♭ The Spirit of the Piece

In order to interpret a piece, the student must first assess the *piece's intention* at every moment. Every piece has a hero, a spirit. At all times, the spirit is making choices, like the choices the student makes in life.

The student must then understand the forces at work either for or against the piece's spirit. These include rhythmic interruptions, changes in mood, harmonic journeys, and other aspects of the musical environment through which the piece's spirit is navigating.

♭ The Piece's Dramatic Paradigm

Neal Bell, the Obie award-winning playwright, said a playwright should never spend stage time "setting up a character," that the character will be shown by her actions. Similarly, the piece's spirit is defined by its actions. It is always working toward a goal. Even Debussy's music, based primarily on moment-to-moment impressions rather than a drive to a harmonic end, has goals. There is always a tonic, an endpoint, a journey to get there, and discoveries made along the way.

This is why various experiments in twentieth-century music often failed to sustain interest over the long term. Modern music often tried to remove any sense of orientation or purpose in a composition, perhaps in an attempt to reflect modern man's isolation and feeling of meaninglessness. In modern styles such as atonality and expressionism, composers eliminated traditional harmonies and often a key center. But no matter what the modern composer did, he could not escape the basic dramatic paradigm of a musical composition. That is, the piece's spirit takes a journey, struggles in some way, and reaches a goal.

The spirit of the piece will change its character over the course of the composition. These changes will depend on the journey and the choices made by the composition's hero. The final situation shows the musical soul's repose.

This dramatic narrative of a musical composition is, of course, affirming. Styles and times may try to beat the soul out of a piece of music, but cannot. The same is true, I believe, in every human.

❧ Prokofiev's "Promenade, opus 65, #1"

This overview shows how this composition's story might be interpreted.

The piece's spirit or hero strolls amiably on a Sunday afternoon. But the first three notes of the right hand outline a bittersweet seventh interval. Signs of unsettled contemplation.

As the B section begins, we see these dark thoughts start to build. The friendly, ambling rhythm of the left hand becomes insistent and off balance, the tonal harmonies that made up its mellow stride now turn strident and neurotic.

Later, the psychological forces are at their highest pitch. When the left-hand ricochets from low to high, the hero literally loses his footing, his grounding. Then the A theme returns, denoting triumph over dark thoughts or simply the ability to accept them as part of everyday settings.

❧ Composer's Life Provides Clues to Interpretation

Both conclusions were true in Prokofiev's life. Choosing to reside in the Soviet Union out of love for his homeland, he was forced by Stalin to write in easily understood musical styles, receiving death threats when he ventured too far into modernism. For someone who had lived in freewheeling Paris and longed to write in contemporary idioms, this kind of artistic schizophrenia must have seemed a daily surrealistic nightmare.

Relating the piece to the composer's life and times gives the student a historical and psychological context for the life of the piece.

§ Student Looks Within

In addition to examining the piece's heroes and anti-heroes and their stories, the student must also look at himself. He must decide how he will nuance the story based on his own character and psychology.

In the Prokofiev piece, the student may decide that the "storm" is more of a distracted daydream, or it could a bit darker. His view of the composition's psychological timbre will depend on his own approach to life. My student, whose picture depicted Saint-Saens' *The Swan* as shot and bleeding, has, not surprisingly, a very serious demeanor.

§ Moment to Moment

Constantin Stanislavski, the great Russian director who developed method acting, taught actors to act out simple motions in rehearsal, developing the body language and emotional reactions that were appropriate to the task. Before the actor ever got to see a script, she had to "live" the character in rehearsal, improvising motions and whole scenes.

Let's say the motion was this: coming in from the rain with an umbrella. The actor had to consider just what someone would do in this situation. First of all, Stanislavski might have asked, "How badly is it raining?" If it's a drizzle, the actor might simply close the umbrella and come in. But in a monsoon, he would fight with the wind, grimace and plan to have the least time with the umbrella down, to avoid getting wet. And what if the house is your new lover's? Perhaps he would walk backward into the house, so as to remain as dry as possible, and carefully close the umbrella so as to not get the hallway wet. On and on they would rehearse, questioning and reacting differently. Actors at his time, the early decades of the twentieth century, were not used to this level of detail. They often used broad gestures, one-size-fits-all motions. Of course we now see the fruits of Stanislavski's work; much of our modern theater and cinema was built on his principles of awareness and sensitivity.

I encourage students to play their pieces with this same attention to detail. What is happening at this moment in the piece's story? How are we reacting?

By listening carefully to the story of the composition, studying the details, and just as importantly, listening to their own psychology and gut-level intuition, students can truthfully portray the life of a composition.

More importantly, they can learn about life's struggles through the endless dramas depicted in great repertoire.

As I Live, So I Practice

❧ Acknowledge All Aspects Of Life

I practice as I live. If I run through the piece and don't correct errors or stop in one section to work on making it beautiful, it is like living life as a fool, not learning from mistakes, not creating beauty, always running, laughing, and taking from life easy pleasures.

If I stop and work too much on one section, and drill over and over, only for discipline, it is like living life with a certain dryness, a brutality, nearsighted and only for gain, either material or in skills. There must be joy in my practice, just as I must have love and wonder in my life.

I must also realize that practice is quite often repetition and fashioning, ever sculpting. It is the slow and methodical effort that will result in performances of great power and understanding. But the performance will only come after long periods of hard work and thought.

This is also true in life. Most of life is work, building opportunities and understanding, sharpening our insight, and working for those moments that come along that transcend the ordinary. They don't come as often as the ordinary, by definition.

I must notice in my pieces where there is beauty, where there is drama, where there is grace, and where there must be work. As in life, I must acknowledge these moments and pay their spirits respect. In this way my soul will grow.

❧ Practicing Piano as Practice for Life

There is a rewarding corollary to thoughtful practice. As I learn to practice wisely, I will also learn to live better. Then the understanding I gain in pieces will help me live more richly. The moments of nobility in Beethoven, of exhilaration and tragedy in Mozart, of grace in Chopin, will make me understand these qualities in life.

❧ Prayer and Faith

In this way, and in others, practice is like prayer. It is a repetitious daily ritual, with some moments of transcendence and rapture, and many more moments of questioning.

There are some moments of doubt. These are often what make us stop practicing for a time, or practice like a fool. Moments of doubt in life can make us depressed, withdraw from life, or act rashly, taking up addictions or destructive lifestyles based on gratification.

If the moments of doubt become too great, if we don't believe we will meet the high moments in our playing, it is possible to stop practicing altogether. This is like a crisis of faith in life.

If I stop practicing, it is like I have committed suicide. I must continue to live, through obstacles, darkness, tragedies, and temporary losses of faith. To do this, and to try to live with proper spirit, is the highest expression of faith.

For this reason, I practice with the belief that obstacles will be overcome. If I am having trouble with them I can go to a guide. A teacher, a CD, a concert, master class or seminar can be my guide.

Practice, like prayer and living, must always start with an abiding faith. This faith can never be in question.

It is not possible, if practice is done in proper spirit, to make our faith in practicing dependent upon outcome. The faith is the premise with which we start and finish. All practice must come from this faith.

In this way, we can improve and stay alive musically.

OUR BUTTERFLIES

If I let myself see and hear them, faces, voices and defining moments from my past surround me.

The woman who took one lesson and dropped,
her face tense and drained from post-partem anxiety.

An adult student who said I was too meticulous and dropped and now I see him around town, looking worried in grocery stores.

The widower's scared face after buying a new Steinway and realizing he was alone with a large "pet" in his limited living room.

My own face as a stranger in strange madly bare spaces playing peaceful Mozart.

An adult student with a broken pinky that pointed at an odd angle who angered easily and exasperated me.

My oak tree thanking me for pruning it. My garden thanking me for marrying my wife.

My wife's quizzical face at the Hong Kong airport after we first met on email.

My own grateful realization over coffee that weekend that she was in fact my wife.

This book is meant as a missive of acceptance for what has led us here, and of the possibilities that remain. I hope it can be a departure point to other gardens, in our minds, hearts and teaching.

Also that by writing this
I can help the gentle reader and myself
Become kinder and closer to
All of our moments and associates

As colorful creatures

Some dark, bold, some brilliant
Some of lighter hue
Some flying high, some out of sight
Some still on the stalk

Crowding our minds and heart
And lifting me with them
On their eventual and inevitable flight.

GLOSSARY FOR TRANSFORMATION

Following are words used throughout the book. A longer list can be found at releasethebutterfly.com. Please add your ideas to the list.

Active Love The practice of extending love to all students based on our past experience in love is called active love. If "love is a decision" is true for one person, it is especially relevant for many.

Balance Point The point that the student is at in understanding, ability, psychology. It is important for the teacher to find the balance point and address it to maintain progress.

Egg Stage The point that we are now at, as pianists, students and teachers. We can assess our position, accept it and then imagine where we want to go.

Fundamental Pulse The perfect rhythm within all humans that resonates with nature. Students and teachers need to penetrate layers of interruption (physical and spiritual habits and other distractions) to access their fundamental pulse.

Layers of Interruption Physical and spiritual habits and other distractions that keep us from hearing and feeling the fundamental pulse.

Lesson Peace The overall emotional, psychological, energy, intellectual, pedagogical, musical, artistic and spiritual balance in a lesson. If the teacher and student have still mind and are connecting to each other and the music, then lesson peace is possible.

Mistake A unique idea in its infancy.

Native Language Fluency An analogy, the point of which is: it is possible to acquire musical skills not inherited at birth.

Personal Rhythm Each pianist, student and teacher has a personal relationship with the temporal aspect of life. Sometimes our personal rhythms can keep us from hearing our fundamental pulse and connecting to the personal rhythm of a composition. But they also show our personality.

Primary Sound Senses Touch and hearing.

Psychic Noise Negative emotions and intrusions on our still mind.

Psychoharmonics The perception of harmonic events (chords, broken chords and other articulations of harmony) as expressions of psychological and emotional states.

Sacred Objects Aspects of our teaching, including facial expressions, tone of voice, various techniques or "tricks," and actual objects that we use to empower students.

Secondary Sound Senses Sight, taste and smell.

Sensory Helper Words Words that evoke certain sensorial reactions. Please see the Thesaurus of Sensory Helper Words, at releasethebutterfly.com for a list of these words and phrases.

Shared Energy Field The combined energies of two people in a closed space. It consists of their emotional states, health, personal rhythm, body size and posture, relative position in room and what happens between them. The shared energy field can be modified by affecting any of these factors, to improve lesson peace.

Sound A pianist's sound is her total sensorial relationship with the music.

Spiritual Habit Any spiritual issue that gets in the way of a pianist's healthy technique, musicmaking or living.

Still Mind A pianist, student or teacher will achieve still mind when she can manage negative emotions and other mental intrusions. When that happens, there can be peace in the lesson and in our practice, and progress is possible.

Travel To move along the keyboard. I find during lessons that this shorthand saves time and ear space.

True Voice The voice within every willing student that calls out from amidst the chaos that sometimes is learning and change. We must always try to hear, help uncover and teach to the student's true voice.

Turnaround A pianist, piano student or teacher who holds preconceived notions about herself and after a time, gains freedom from these notions.

Whole thinking A possible substitute for the word "holistic."

LIST OF PROFESSIONALS

Please see releasethebutterfly.com for available contact information.

Carl C. Atteniese, Jr., Poet, Artist, Teacher, and Zen Compassionist; Publisher of Ukiway Journal on the web

Tina Awad, LMT, BFA

Alexei Bukreev, Professor of the Ural State Conservatory in Yekaterinburg

Ruth Ehrenberg, M.Ed., Lic SW, Psychotherapist and Instructor in Music Appreciation

Gregory Burnham, Chief Technology Officer, Port Authority of New York and New Jersey

Mary Carlino, Fashion Design Consultant

Anna Choi, Instructor in Violin

Rudy Cypser, Chairman of CURE, New York and lead facilitator for Alternatives to Violence workshops

Mary Greenberg, Instructor in Piano, Westminster Conservatory, Princeton, New Jersey

Amy Greer, Piano Department Head at Powers Music School in Belmont, Massachusetts

Grace E. Jackson, M.D., Psychiatrist, Lecturer, and Family Practice Resident

Mary Sue Laing, M.Ed., Remedial Teacher

Suzanne Little, Ph.D., Director, Mind/Body Program Continuum Center for Health and Healing; Assistant Clinical Professor of Psychiatry and Behavioral Sciences, Albert Einstein College of Medicine

Jimmy Mack, owner of Jimmy's Barber Shop, Princeton, New Jersey

Adelaide B. McKelway, Instructor in Piano, formerly with Davidson College in North Carolina

Isabelle Mackiewicz-Elden, BFRP, Bach Foundation Registered Practitioner, Bach Flower Therapy

Barbara Mannas, formerly secretary at OXFAM

Dr. Alexandra Mascolo-David, Associate Professor of Piano at Central Michigan University

Dr. Alan Mason, Associate Professor of Music, Barry University, Florida

Lewis Mehl-Madrona, M.D., Author of Coyote Healing; Faculty, Program in Integrative Medicine, University of Arizona

Raghu Murthy, M.D., Retina Specialist and Ophthalmologist

Alison Neely, Instructor in Piano, Westminster Conservatory, Princeton, New Jersey

Laurie Powsner, MSW, Grief Therapist

Angelo Tuckoo Sargentini, Trainer Guy for Small World
  Coffee, Princeton, New Jersey
Frank Summers, Ph.D., Training and Supervising Analyst,
  Chicago Institute for Psychoanalysis
Grace Ting, M.D., Emergency Medicine
Richard Thorpe, M.D., Emergency Medicine
Alyson Ward, Instructor in Piano

About the Author

Bob Diefendorf teaches piano in Princeton, New Jersey, at the Westminster Conservatory of Music.

He is married to Penni, who taught him how to be happy.

His students taught him how to see the world upside down and he thanks them.

Not long ago he learned how to drive and is glad that he never drove when young because he would never have gotten out of the car.

He loves Hong Kong especially when it is brown or black level rain or higher.

He believes that to ignore the infinite possibilities of peace is to ignore the essence of America, that of infinite possibility.

He has written many songs and compositions for students. Some are undiscovered masterpieces, others are simply undiscovered.

He is founder and president of Small Miracles Foundation that provides free music lessons to children in need. He hopes that someday soon the idea that children will ever be in need, for music lessons, school or anything else will be archaic.

He hopes that naivete will come back in style especially where it relates to politics, religion and human kindness.

He and Penni love karaoke.

He is working on several other books and musicals, some even outside of his mind.

He is in love with the souls of about 743 people but they'll never know unless they catch his eye.

For many years he felt alive only while teaching, especially music history in the Young Artist program, but now feels alive most of the time.

He hopes you disagree with most of this book and write your own. Then he will have succeeded.

He doesn't usually speak in third person.